BOOST your CREATIVITY

ROBERT ALLEN

BOOST your **CREATIVITY**

COLLINS & BROWN

First published in Great Britain in 2005 by Collins & Brown Ltd

The Chrysalis Building,

Bramley Road,

London W10 6SP

An imprint of **Chrysalis** Books Group plc

Design: Zoe Mellors

Project Editor: Nicola Hodgson

Editorial Assistant: Carly Madden

10 9 8 7 6 5 4 3 2 1

British Library Cataloguing-in-Publication Data:

A catalogue record for this book is available from the British Library.

ISBN 1 84340 242 4

Colour reproduction by Mission Productions Ltd, Hong Kong

Printed and bound by SNP, Lee Fung, China

CONTENTS

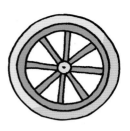

PART ONE:
THE BASICS

The power of creativity is available to all of us. It is one human characteristic that everyone shares, though some are better at making use of it than others. The exercises and techniques that follow are designed to help you train yourself to get the maximum benefit from your own creativity.

Creativity is not limited to any one area of life. It plays a part in art, science, problem solving, cookery, sport, music and hundreds of other activities. But no matter what your chosen field of endeavour is you will find that by training your creative powers you will enhance your ability and greatly increase your chances of success.

'Imagination is the living power and prime agent of all human perception.'

SAMUEL TAYLOR COLERIDGE

 LOOK FOR THE LIGHTBULB SYMBOL.
It is there to highlight bright ideas that will help you boost your creative abilities.

WHAT IS CREATIVITY?

Creativity is the divine spark. It is the nearest we humans get to playing God and, if you miss out on it, you are missing one of the best experiences a human can have (and yes, sex – that other favourite human experience – is directly linked to our creative urge).

At its best, creativity involves putting an idea where before there was just a blank. Some of the greatest artists and scientists in history have done this and made themselves immortal – there will never be another Michelangelo or Galileo; their contributions were unique. But creativity does not have to be of this outstanding quality in order to be valuable. We all have the power to dream up something new and exciting, or even to take an existing idea and put a fresh gloss on it in such a way that it becomes revitalized.

This book is based on the simple proposition that each and every one of us is capable of enormous creative output, yet in far too many cases, we do not realize it and our ability remains unexploited. Schools are usually geared to producing identically educated units; creativity is quirky and unpredictable. It is therefore small wonder that although the educational machine pays lip service to creativity, in reality it avoids it (except in the less academic subjects, such as art).

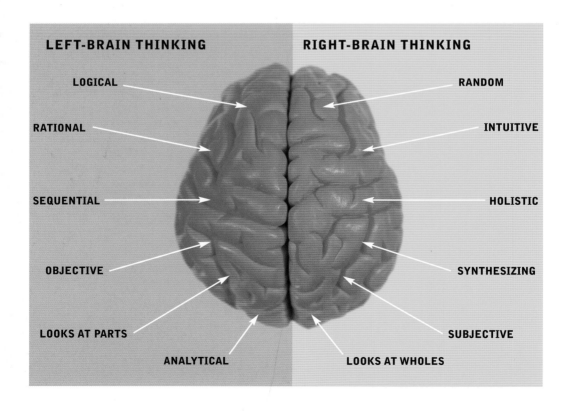

LEFT-BRAIN THINKING	RIGHT-BRAIN THINKING
LOGICAL	RANDOM
RATIONAL	INTUITIVE
SEQUENTIAL	HOLISTIC
OBJECTIVE	SYNTHESIZING
LOOKS AT PARTS	SUBJECTIVE
ANALYTICAL	LOOKS AT WHOLES

A BRAIN OF TWO HALVES

How does creativity come about? Tests have shown that the two hemispheres of the brain are each responsible for a different manner of thought. The illustration demonstrates the differences between left- and right-brain thinking.

Most individuals display a distinct preference for using one side of the brain. Some, however, are equally adept at both modes. In general, schools tend to concentrate on boosting their students' left-brain abilities in 'scholastic' subjects that rely on logical thinking, analysis and accuracy. Right-brain subjects, on the other hand, focus on aesthetics, feelings and creativity (and tend to be downplayed in traditional academic environments). The right brain is the place where creative ideas are born and therefore it is in our interests to stimulate that area of the brain. This can be done by attempting tasks that need a bit of imagination and benefit from a fresh approach. The left brain, however, is not to be despised. Once a bright idea is born we need the logical, analytical skills of the left brain to help translate the idea into something practical that will work in the real world.

This book will help you to find out where you fit on the left-brain/right-brain continuum; it will show you how to increase your creativity, and consequently enhance your life and career.

THE TELEPHONE TEST

This is a quick way of working out whether you are predominantly left- or right-brained. How do you hold a telephone? Strangely, your ears are cross-wired to your brain – your left ear is connected to your right brain, and vice versa. Therefore, if you normally hold the phone to your left ear, your preference is for right-brain activity, whereas using the right ear marks you as an analytical left-brainer.

CREATIVE, OR JUST PLAIN NUTS?

Being creative is all about thinking in unconventional ways. See if you can see beyond the obvious to solve this problem.

A man was driving to town when he had a flat tyre. He changed the wheel, but in one of those 'Why does this always happen to me?' moments, four of the five wheel nuts rolled down a drain. How could he continue his journey without calling a mechanic for assistance?

⊙ Answer on page 122.

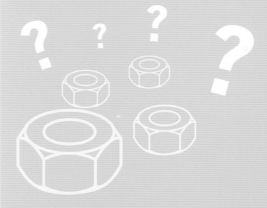

WHAT QUALIFIES AS CREATIVITY?

Creativity is very much in vogue at the moment, but this has not always been the case. There have been many periods in history when it was considered right and proper to follow traditional ideas, and any sort of innovation was seen as disrespectful and potentially troublesome.

But our age is one of rapid change and the constant flowering of new ideas. This is almost universally acknowledged to be a Good Thing, although often we only have a vague idea of what we mean by it. For example, are an innovative new novelist and a person who invents a new type of vacuum cleaner both creative? If you have bright ideas for decorating your bedroom are you as creative as the person who invents a cure for a deadly disease?

We use the word 'creativity' in such a wide variety of contexts that it has become very hard to define what we really mean by it. Some feel that the word should only properly be used for major new developments in serious areas such as the arts and sciences. Even then, there is often a huge amount of disagreement over whether a particular idea is creative or not. How many times have you heard certain critics rave over an experimental new work while others condemn it as rubbish?

THE CREATIVE GENIUS

There are really two major divisions in creativity. The first is the province of the geniuses and visionaries. People of the calibre of Albert Einstein, William Shakespeare, Wolfgang Amadeus Mozart, Isaac Newton, Pablo Picasso and Leonardo da Vinci all have one thing in common: they invented entirely new ideas and pushed human thought to new

PICASSO is important because he took painting to a new level and made people think in unfamiliar ways.

limits. Very few of us will ever join that select company and it would be idle to pretend that creativity of that order can be taught. Geniuses are born, not made. There is, however, a secondary level of creativity in which existing knowledge is presented in new, exciting and stimulating ways. Just because this sort of creativity does not involve works of genius, that is no reason to despise it. Many of the most valuable developments in human progress have resulted from an imaginative use of existing ideas. The vast majority of ideas that people consider to be creative will come within this second group. Most of us have bright ideas from time to time and, with a little practice, we can train ourselves to have more and more of them.

JOE PUBLIC, CREATOR EXTRAORDINAIRE

The good news is that this type of creativity is common in all areas of human endeavour. There is simply nothing that we do that cannot be done better. The improvement and refinement of ideas is something that people do as a matter of course. Think, for example, of the progress that has been made since the invention of the telephone. In a very short time it has gone from being a large, unwieldy piece of apparatus owned only by the wealthy, to something small enough to slip into a pocket and that is cheap enough for children to own.

Creativity can often be a team effort, too. We tend to think of the creative person as a solitary pioneer; we like the image of the wayward genius who wows the world with a ground-breaking new idea. But the truth is that much creativity is the result of many people applying their minds to a common problem.

WHY ARE HUMANS SPECIAL?

Creativity is a human characteristic. While other creatures possess many remarkable abilities – they can fly, run faster than us, hear better than us and have a much more developed sense of smell – they will never be able to learn to create in the very special way that humans do.

BOUNDLESS CURIOSITY

We are amazingly curious about the world around us. Cats may be a byword for curiosity, but the cat is a mere dullard when compared to even the stupidest human. Humans want to know everything. We don't explore merely because it might help us to find extra food, or to defend our territory against enemies – we explore for the pure joy of it. We always want to know how things work, why things happen in the way they do and what lies over the horizon. This curiosity on its own would constitute a powerful weapon, but allied to other abilities, it turns into something truly amazing.

ABSTRACT THOUGHT

Humans have the ability to understand abstract concepts. We can use ideas in a way that other species cannot. Even people who are not 'thinkers' have no trouble with concepts such as truth, justice or honesty. The power to deal in abstract ideas has led to some remarkable human achievements – for example, Einstein's Theory of Relativity. Although most people have no idea what

relativity is all about, it does not alter the fact that certain humans with a highly developed capacity for abstract thought are able to entertain ideas of astonishing complexity.

UNSTOPPABLE CREATIVITY

Creativity is a fundamental part of our nature. We constantly search for new ways to do things, and for new things to do. Take spiders, for example. They have been building webs in the same way for millions of years. Have any of them thought of turning the thing on its side and using it as a trampoline? Of course not. Have any of them considered that by twanging the threads it might possibly work as a musical instrument? Again, the answer is no. Would humans have had these thoughts? You bet! Humans are inventors and problem-solvers. We constantly try out new ideas just for the fun of it. Many of the ideas don't work, but that never bothers us because eventually we will find one that does.

FAVOURABLE CONDITIONS

Animals struggle to live. They not only have to compete for food and shelter, but they must also keep an eye out for predators. In the wild, the overwhelming majority don't even live long enough to reach sexual maturity. By comparison, humans (even those in poor countries) live lives of great security. In prosperous countries, we live in a way that previous generations would have marvelled at. We have no predators, food is plentiful and homes are not hard to come by. There

are two main consequences that flow from this. Firstly, we have the luxury of being able to devote huge amounts of energy to matters that have no immediate survival value (art and literature, for example). Secondly, we increasingly live to a great age. Once our lives as parents are over, we are by no means a spent force and have many years of productive existence ahead of us.

CREATIVE SURGES

One of the most exciting facts about creativity is that it breeds more creativity. For example, we are constantly finding better and faster means to communicate with each other. Not so very long ago, communication was quite slow and inefficient – there were no computers, no mobile phones, and TV broadcasts were confined to the evenings. If you wanted to communicate with someone in another part of the country or overseas, you would probably write a letter. Nowadays, everyone keeps in touch by phone and the

internet. In terms of creativity, this means that minds all over the world can be brought to focus on a single project with great ease. A team with members in, say, America, Australia, England, Italy and Japan can achieve an immediacy of communication that belies the fact that they are on different continents. This ease of communication, which is in itself the product of creative energy, is the means by which further creative leaps will take place.

CREATIVE TIP
Ask 'Why?' constantly.
All creativity stems from
questioning why things are the way
they are. The more everyday and obvious a
thing is, the more it needs to be questioned.

HOW CAN CREATIVITY BE JUDGED?

In all areas of activity, we need some means of assessing the quality of what is being achieved; creativity is no different. When faced with new ideas of any sort, there are several questions that will enable us to decide whether the ideas are genuinely important or only of passing interest.

IS THIS A NEW IDEA?

As we have already discussed, genuinely new ideas are rare, and it is only occasionally that people of genius come up with something entirely new. Quite often, such ideas are so revolutionary that very few people can actually grasp them and their implications. Therefore we might only be able to give a provisional answer to this question, or have to defer the whole issue to a future time when we are better able to make a judgement.

IS IT A GENUINE IMPROVEMENT?

Some ideas may look good but, on closer inspection, are really no better than what we already have. Mere novelty is not enough to qualify an idea as being creative. For example, look at the humble corkscrew. The basic implement is simple, practical and cheap. Over the years, people have come up with a huge variety of 'improvements' that use complicated systems of leverage, or that depend on injecting compressed gas into the bottle.

Some of these newer versions work quite well, but none has ever succeeded in making the original design obsolete. If you go to any restaurant, you will find that wine waiters still prefer to use a corkscrew of the traditional design.

DOES THE BENEFIT OUTWEIGH THE COST?

Any new idea, however brilliant, will entail an element of cost. The idea will only catch on if the cost is proportionate to the benefit derived from it. The earliest form of the light bulb, for example, was far too expensive, especially since it had a very short lifespan. It was only when light bulbs became cheap and long-lasting that the use of electric lighting caught on.

WILL IT BE CAPABLE OF FURTHER IMPROVEMENT?

This is a tricky one. Some ideas are so good that they last forever in their original form – for example the mousetrap, an idea that is simple, cheap and effective. Some ideas, however, are good because they can be developed. The computer is a recent example.

Thirty years ago, a computer was a huge piece of apparatus that needed its own air-conditioned room. Only laboratories and businesses could afford one. But the computer was an idea that could be developed endlessly. It got smaller, faster and cheaper so rapidly that it has been hard to keep up with the rate of progress. No sooner do you buy one than it is obsolete. This is one of the best examples of creativity at work.

WILL IT STAND THE TEST OF TIME?

When we judge creativity, an important consideration is whether a new idea will have staying power. Is it a passing fad or will it be with us for generations to come? When will the wheel be replaced by something better? Never. This is one example of an idea that, although incredibly ancient and simple, is unlikely ever to be bettered. Some new ideas are popular for a short time but eventually fall from favour. Others might be valuable for some time but are eventually superseded by an even better idea. In all fields of human activity, we come across examples of genius that will never be surpassed, such as the plays of Shakespeare or the music of Mozart. But what about, for example, Einstein's Theory of Relativity? Scientific ideas are in a different category because, however brilliant a theory may be, it is likely that as our understanding deepens, it will be replaced.

THE EXTRAORDINARY HISTORY OF THE WHEEL

The wheel is a good example of an idea that has been capable of endless adaptation. Archaeologists believe that the earliest form of the wheel was not, as one might believe, developed from the rollers that were used to move heavy objects. Instead, it was probably originated by potters and made from planks nailed together. It is even possible that the first wheel was in fact square! But once the basic idea had been developed, there was no limit to the uses that could be found for it. Not only did it make many forms of transport possible, but it also appeared, in numerous guises, in machinery. There can be few ideas that are so simple but that have had such enormous influence on the development of civilization.

CAN YOU LEARN TO BE CREATIVE?

Everybody has the capacity to be creative. As we have seen, the creative urge is something that is uniquely human. Why then do some people produce a constant flow of new ideas and others don't?

Part of the answer is to do with natural ability. Just as some people are good at running, playing chess, swimming or learning languages, others are good at having ideas. But confidence and self-esteem also play a large part in the process.

If you believe that you are creative and that your ideas are valuable, you will be motivated to produce more of them. If, on the other hand, you have never been encouraged to consider yourself capable of producing bright ideas, the likelihood is that you will not produce many and, if you do have an idea, you will automatically assume that it is of no real value. Fear of ridicule and lack of self-esteem are major disabilities in the creative process.

> **CREATIVE TIP**
> Always be suspicious when people say, 'It stands to reason'. Human progress has come from those who had the courage to challenge the generally held view.

GETTING STARTED

If you follow the exercises in this book you will find that you have a creative spark that can be fanned into a flame. Creativity cannot be taught in the way that you can teach, say, maths or science, but it can be encouraged to grow. If you make your mind a fertile ground for good ideas, you will find that they flourish there. You do not need to be a genius, you don't even have to be especially clever, but you do need to open yourself up to the creative spirit that lies within your unconscious mind. Once you start to have ideas, you will generate more; and once your ideas start to be appreciated by other people, you will find yourself motivated to continue developing your creative powers.

> **CREATIVE TIP**
> When working on a problem, never be satisfied with your first solution even if it seems to be correct. Always look for other answers.

HERE ARE SOME THINGS YOU NEED TO DO TO GET STARTED:

Most importantly of all, make a conscious decision that from now on you ARE a creative person.

⦿ In future, all your ideas (however trivial they may seem) have to be collected and kept. You never know when an idea will come in handy, or when something that seemed unimportant when you first thought of it will suddenly become of vital importance.

⦿ Pick some creative projects to get yourself started. It helps to have several projects on the go at the same time, as they tend to cross-fertilize each other. It also helps if the projects are of quite different types.

⦿ Work on your projects regularly and methodically. Don't ever just sit around waiting for inspiration. If one project gets bogged down, turn to another and work on that. Make sure that you set yourself goals and deadlines – if you don't do this, you may find that you run out of steam and fail to finish things you've started.

⦿ Try to keep your attitude as flexible as possible. Your unconscious mind has an agenda of its own and, in order for your efforts to succeed, you need to be prepared to change your plans to accommodate whatever your unconscious prompts you to do.

⦿ Remember to have fun! Creativity is hard work but it is also enjoyable. Don't get so focused on attaining your goal that you forget to enjoy the creative process.

⦿ Remember that having bright ideas, though very important, is only a part of the creative process. Once you have the idea you then have to work hard to bring it to fruition. This is the part of the process that defeats many would-be creative people. They enjoy the processes by which bright ideas are born but lack the energy to see their project through to the end. What a waste of good ideas! Make sure that you are a worker as well as a dreamer.

THE CHARACTERISTICS OF CREATIVE PEOPLE

Creative people have a number of things in common. Not all of them will exhibit every one of the characteristics below but, generally, creative people tend to conform to these descriptions.

1. ENERGY

Creative individuals tend to be energetic. Though they may have bouts of laziness (like most of us), they do manage to overcome this and get things done. They have a deeply felt need to be productive, because they get a strong emotional boost from creative work.

2. CURIOSITY

Creative individuals are very curious. They tend to question everything and try to see the world from new perspectives. Their questioning may sometimes irritate others who are of a more practical turn of mind.

3. IDEAS FOR THEIR OWN SAKE

They love ideas for their own sake. Even if an idea is of no apparent practical value, they will investigate it if it seems interesting enough. However, they can be fickle and will drop an idea in which their interest has waned, even if it means abandoning a project.

4. PUTTING IDEAS INTO PRACTICE

They often enjoy making things. This can manifest itself in all sorts of ways, but they always get a great deal of satisfaction from seeing an idea turned into a finished product. Again, they can be fickle and suddenly get bored with a project before it is brought to a conclusion.

5. PLAYFULNESS

They are often playful and quite happy to mess about with activities that others might regard as childish. They are not especially bothered about appearing serious or adult.

6. IMAGINATION AND FANTASY

Creative individuals are very adept at using imagination and fantasy; they also have a strong desire to use the things they dream up as a basis for projects. They are far more concerned about using an interesting idea than producing a practical outcome.

7. FOCUSING ON PROJECTS

As long as the ideas they are using remain sufficiently arresting, creative people are able to remain focused on a project for as long as it takes to bring it to a successful conclusion. They can be quite obsessive and frequently become deeply involved in a project.

CREATIVE TIP
Multi-tasking is very good for creativity. If you work on several things at the same time, you will find that the projects have a way of helping each other along.

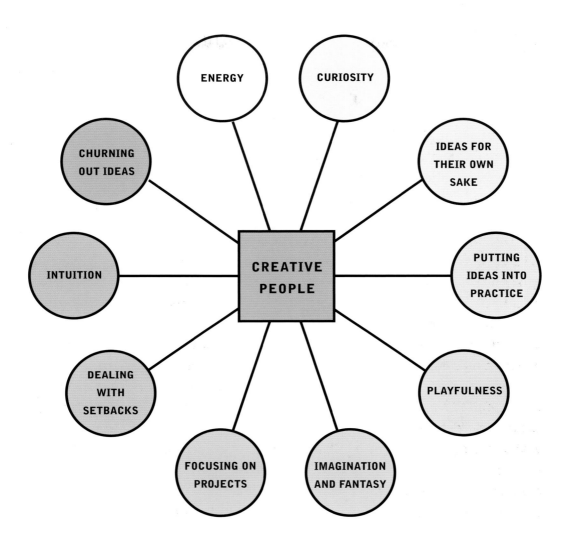

8. DEALING WITH SETBACKS

They are very resilient and not easily put off by setbacks. For them, the most important thing is to continue to create at all costs.

9. INTUITION

Creative people are closely in touch with the promptings of their unconscious. They are very intuitive and tend to feel their way to solutions rather than work them out logically.

However, they may well need others to help with the nitty-gritty of their projects, as they are prone to overlook practicalities and irritating details.

10. CHURNING OUT IDEAS

Creative people are more interested in having ideas than in exploiting them. They are often quite happy to leave the development phase to others.

HOW CREATIVE AM I?

People who have not had much chance to put their creativity to use often wonder whether they possess such a faculty at all.

It is quite common to hear people say, 'I'm not very creative. I never have any good ideas.' This is simply not true. If you're human, you are creative – because creativity is fundamental to human life. We can't help being creative any more than a fish can help swimming. However, people frequently fail to recognize and nurture their creative faculties. Try this simple test. Look at the pictures below for a couple of minutes and then make up a story that involves them all. The story needn't be a great work of literature – you can make it as simple as you wish. Take the pictures in any order you like.

CREATIVE TIP
Never worry about ideas that don't work.
Most ideas are like that. Just be encouraged
to keep trying for a better idea.

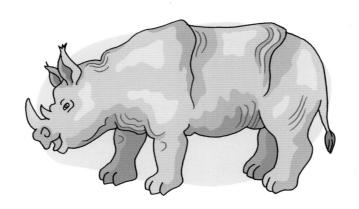

HOW DID YOU GET ON?

My guess is that you managed to come up with a story – no matter how wild and wacky – that linked all the pictures within a few minutes. Storytelling is a major creative faculty. It serves not only to entertain, but also helps us to explore the nature of the world around us, sort out our problems and vicariously experience situations that we would probably avoid in real life.

AM I GOOD ENOUGH?

People who wish to make better use of their creative powers are often put off by the thought that they might not be good enough.

I regularly teach creative writing classes, and commonly find that students are shy of using their creative talents because they feel they won't measure up to some preconceived standard of excellence. Interestingly, this sort of fear mainly affects adults – children are much more forthcoming because they have not yet learnt a fear of failure. If you fall into this category, there are a few things you should bear in mind:

VINCENT VAN GOGH sold only one painting during his lifetime but has since been hailed as a genius.

- Nearly everybody starts out by producing creative ideas that are only average. This is only to be expected; you usually have to go through a period of apprenticeship before you start to generate ideas that are really valuable.

- You are not always in the best position to decide how good your work is. It is worth getting independent opinions before you judge yourself too harshly. (On the other hand, never let other people's negative opinions put you off. There are always those who want to discourage newcomers.)

- Remember that even famous creative people were often unaware of the extent of their own talent. Van Gogh sold only one painting during the whole of his life. Shakespeare never managed to give up work as a jobbing actor and live entirely from his writing. Sometimes you have to wait for the judgement of history to decide just how good you were.

The questions opposite will help you to clarify your ideas about your creative ability. There are no right or wrong answers; the questions are designed to get you to assess your own abilities honestly.

ASSESS YOUR CREATIVITY ABILITIES

1. Do you often look for new and better ways to do routine tasks?
2. Do you enjoy activities such as drawing, sculpture, writing and making music?
3. Do you enjoy solving problems?
4. Does your mind constantly produce new ideas even when you aren't really looking for them?
5. Do you enjoy making things?
6. Do you have a good eye for colour?
7. Do you like playing with abstract ideas just for the fun of it?
8. When you tell people about things that have happened to you, do you embroider the narrative so that it becomes a story rather than a purely factual account?
9. Do you enjoy trying new experiences?
10. Do you cook and, if so, do you enjoy trying or inventing new recipes?
11. Do you enjoy gardening?
12. Do you often have new ideas for decorating your home?
13. Do you enjoy playing with words (making puns or creating anagrams, for example)?
14. Do you make music all the time by humming, whistling or improvising percussion?
15. Do you find that taking part in creative activities makes you feel happier?

WHAT IT MEANS

- If you answered 'Yes' to all or most of the questions, your creative urge is particularly strong. The techniques taught in this book will help you to develop your abilities and make the best of them.

- If you answered 'Yes' to over half the questions, your creative abilities are quite strong but could do with a bit of a boost. The activities in the rest of the book will help you uncover some abilities that you didn't know you had.

- If you answered 'Yes' to only a few of the questions, your creative abilities are blocked for some reason. The exercises that follow should help you to remove that block and fully access your creative powers.

CREATIVE TIP
Always carry a notebook for jotting down any bright ideas that you may have. Ideas come to the surface all the time but, unless they are quickly caught, will often escape and you may well find that you are quite unable to remember them later.

PART TWO:
THE SEVEN STEPS TO CREATIVITY

This is the part of the book that will challenge your brain to come up with some bright ideas. The tests and exercises all depend on your being able to think beyond the obvious and find a solution that is not immediately apparent to the logical part of your mind.

Creativity can happen in unpredictable ways but it can help to think of it in seven steps. Step 1 involves abandoning traditional thinking in favour of new methods and solutions. Step 2 examines how ideas that at first seem crazy can make huge contributions to our progress. Step 3 looks at that strange area of the mind that exists on the border between waking and sleep. Step 4 deals with the creative power that can be generated by apparently random thoughts. Step 5 examines the role of the unconscious mind. Step 6 looks at the contribution of other facets of the mind. Finally, Step 7 examines the long and often painstaking process by which a bright idea is brought to fruition as a creative project.

'An invasion of armies can be resisted, but not an idea whose time has come.'

VICTOR HUGO

LEARNING TO 'THINK OUTSIDE THE BOX'

From an early age, we are taught to think in a certain way: to be rational, to do what has been done before and not to defy convention.

Subliminally, we're also taught to follow the crowd, not to take chances and to trust neither our instincts nor our imagination (which, after all, only produces 'flights of fancy' that get us nowhere). It consequently becomes an ingrained habit to look for solutions to problems by referring to what has been done before.

This way of thinking is a 'box' that hinders our ability to think creatively. We end up doing what military leaders tend to do (as observed by military historians) – they develop tactics that would have brought a speedy triumph in the most recently fought war but that prove to be useless when applied to the next war that comes along. Also, the brain itself is wired to think in certain ways – this, too, is a 'box'. To think creatively, we need to get out of both boxes. Do these two exercises to start the journey and find out how boxy your brain is!

ORIGINAL THINKER

This test will surprise you. It shows very clearly how our brains are wired in certain ways. When you have done it yourself, try it out on family and friends to see if their response is the same.

Complete the following calculations:

$$1 + 5 =$$
$$7 - 1 =$$
$$4 + 2 =$$
$$8 - 2 =$$
$$3 + 3 =$$
$$0 + 6 =$$

- Now repeat the word 'six' out loud for about fifteen seconds.

- Look at the panel at the bottom of the page.

NAME A VEGETABLE

➡ Now look at the panel on page 62

TESTING YOUR ORIGINALITY OF THOUGHT

This game demonstrates your ability to think outside the box, but only if you give yourself time. Have a good, long look at the eight small images below. What could they be? There is no single correct answer. In fact, the more answers you can come up with, the better. Take your time, because the longer you take, the more likely you are to get new and better ideas. Once you've had a good look at all eight images, use the scoring system explained below to see how well you've done.

There is no time limit on this task.

- The first time you attempt this task give yourself one point for each idea you come up with. At the end of the task add up your total number of points and see how well you did.

  10–15 = poor
  16–40 = average
  41–60 = good
  above 60 = excellent

- Return to the task a little later (next day, for example) and try again. This time, give yourself three points for each new idea. Again, tot up your final score and measure your originality of thought using the following scoring system.

  9–12 = poor
  15–24 = average
  27–36 = good
  above 36 = excellent

- Finally, come back to the test a week later and have one last go. This is the most exciting part of the test. By now, you should be right out of ideas; everything that 'makes sense' will have occurred to you long ago. On the other hand, your mind will have been turning over the problem subconsciously. This time, give yourself five points per idea.

  0–15 = poor
  20–30 = average
  35–50 = good
  over 50 = excellent

As you will have noticed, once you had exhausted all the 'rational' options and were forced to use your imagination (and had started to think outside the box in a more creative way), many more possibilities will have sprung to mind!

OBSTACLES TO CREATIVE THINKING

One of the worst enemies of creative thinking is the dangerous habit of relying on old-style thinking to tackle a new problem. This is very seductive, because it produces a known result at a predictable cost.

Young people, who by definition haven't got much experience of anything, are inclined to think out a problem from scratch. Their elders, however, make up for their relatively slower thought processes by relying on experience. And what is experience? It's remembering the thing that worked last time. This is a disaster for creativity. It means that all the thinking within an organization ends up running on rail tracks laid by the oldest and most senior managers. The room for creative solutions is very limited or, sometimes, non-existent.

Now you may be thinking, 'How stupid to let things carry on like that. If I were in charge, I'd encourage the young people to come up with wonderful creative solutions.' The trouble is that many new ideas simply don't work. The unconscious mind is excellent at producing an endless supply of ideas but these come with no guarantee of quality. In fact, the vast majority of new ideas simply don't work. To rely on new thinking to solve a problem is therefore expensive and has an uncertain outcome. If you hit a winner, you may do very well, but what if all the bright ideas that your bright young managers come up with turn out to be duds? Then you face an expensive failure, for which senior management will eventually have to carry the can. This is why people tend to play safe and go for ideas that are tried and tested.

There are many ways in which our capacity for creative thinking is reduced or even eliminated. Let's look at some of them.

THE MONKEY TRAP

This famous story is often used to illustrate a problem with creative thinking. The monkey trap is a simple device that depends, for its effectiveness, on the limited thinking powers of the monkey. A hollowed-out coconut is hung from a tree. A small hole is made in the bottom of the coconut and a tempting snack is placed inside. Here's the clever bit: the hole is just big enough for the monkey to slide in his open hand, but not big enough for him to withdraw his closed fist.

The monkey smells the food, puts his hand into the hole, grasps the food and then can't pull his clenched fist through the opening. When the hunters arrive, the monkey panics, and because he is not thinking clearly, he still tries to pull his closed fist through the hole. Nothing is holding him prisoner except his own defective thinking.

THINKING THE UNTHINKABLE

Here is another story about problems with thinking. Two little boys are playing table

tennis, when their one and only ball falls into a small hole in the floor. It is a very snug fit and there is no room for the boys to get their fingers around the ball to pull it out. They are afraid they will get into trouble if they confess to having lost the ball, so they cannot call an adult for help. There are no tools in the room. They try blowing into the hole but, although the ball rises when they blow down the side, they aren't able to catch it before it sinks back down again. Eventually, they have another idea and get the ball out of the hole.

If you ask people how this was done, they tend to fall into three groups. There are those who have no idea at all. There are those who do have an idea but are unwilling to propose it. And there are the very few who get the right answer. Why? Because the answer is that one of the kids urinated into the hole and floated the ball to the surface. Gross? Oh, yes. But that is the point. What puts people off seeing the answer is that it calls for them to think something disagreeable. Creative thinking requires us to think the unthinkable.

Here are some factors that contribute to people not thinking creatively:

Habit

Habit is a terrible thing from the point of view of creativity. Unfortunately, it is often perceived as being good, because if you always do what you did the time before, you will find solutions quickly and this will appear to save money – but it is a deeply misguided policy. We need to struggle with new ideas. This is how humans progress; it is how we grow. No amount of short-term benefit can outweigh our need to discover new ideas. The motto of the college I attended was 'Do different'. I'm not usually keen on mottoes, but this is one that I would commend to anyone who wants to think creatively.

Fear

People hate to look stupid. We will do just about anything rather than admit that we don't understand what others are talking about. We keep quiet rather than offer an idea that might be dismissed or, even worse, laughed at. As long as you are afraid of what other people might think, you are never going to be a truly creative person. Creativity is all about doing new things that others will inevitably find strange, stupid or shocking. Unless you have the courage to be a leader rather than a follower, you will never use your creative powers to the full.

Laziness

Being creative sounds like a lot of fun. It is a lot of fun, but it is also a lot of hard work. Having ideas, although difficult enough in itself, is only the start of the process. There will usually be a long, hard road to travel before your idea comes to fruition. Ideas have to be refined and difficulties overcome (and there are always difficulties because nothing ever goes entirely to plan). People tend to be lazy and dislike putting in the sort of long, sustained effort that any creative project requires. As a writer, I can tell you that playing around with the original idea is fun, producing sample material and selling the idea to the publisher is fun, but the long slog of actually writing the book is often no fun at all. So if you want to be creative, you need to reconcile yourself to the idea that you will have to work hard to achieve what you want.

Lack of persistence

An idea, however good, will encounter resistance when it is first proposed. In fact, the more stunning and original an idea, the more resistance it will meet. Therefore, if you want to your idea to succeed, you have to be prepared to push it for all you're worth. People who give up easily will never succeed in any form of creative endeavour.

Thinking about the pay-off

The rewards of creativity sometimes, but by no means always, include money and fame. But if you make these things the main object of your activity, you are unlikely to succeed. Creativity demands your full attention, and it simply won't work as a means to some other end. If, for example, you start out to write a

---

CREATIVE TIP

It is always easier to ask for forgiveness than to ask for permission. If you believe in your idea, you must go ahead with it at all costs. If you wait for permission, it might never come. If you find that you are wrong, admit it frankly and then get on with your next project.

book, you need to make it the very best book you are capable of writing, and not the one you think will get you the most attention.

DIGGING A HOLE

Here is another reason that people fail to think creatively. Imagine that you are asked to dig a hole. After a short time of digging, you have achieved a circular hole about 1 m (3.2 ft) deep. If someone then came along and said, 'Sorry, I've changed my mind, it should be dug over there', you wouldn't be too upset.

Now, after a lot of work, the hole is 3 m (7.8 ft) deep. Would you be so keen to start again if the same thing happened? No, you wouldn't. You'd be quite annoyed.

Let's say that you carry on digging. The hole is now 25 m (82 ft) deep. You have hired people to help and you have employed a mining engineer to advise on how to shore up the hole and keep it from collapsing. By now it is your hole. You are responsible for its size and shape. You are responsible for the workers on the project and they are relying on you to keep them in a job. Do you see what is happening? You have now invested so much time, energy, thought and money in this project that you would be traumatized if it were suddenly scrapped.

Now, imagine that the hole is really a piece of scientific research, a book you have been writing, a painting you have spent months on or an invention you have been

> ### CREATIVE TIP
> Take a random word – the more ridiculous the better – and try to find a way to work it into your creative project. This exercise may seem tough and you might not see right away how it will help but if you persist you'll be surprised at the number of original notions that suddenly pop into your mind.

trying to get marketed. You can see why people are often unwilling to think things that will rock the boat, and why they will also resist anyone who comes along and tries to criticize the project with which they are so intimately involved.

LATERAL THINKING

The term 'lateral thinking' was coined by Edward de Bono. He offered various definitions of it, but the most striking was this: 'You cannot dig a hole in a different place by digging the same hole deeper.'

Conventional thinking plods ever onwards in only one direction, but lateral thinking tries to get a new perspective on a problem that shows it to you in an entirely different light.

Puzzles that require you to solve a problem by lateral thinking have long been popular because they allow the solver to indulge a taste for wacky, off-the-wall thinking. Someone with a good imagination and an original turn of mind is far more likely to excel at problems of this sort than someone who tries to apply conventional logic. Try solving the problems in this section and see whether you can liberate your thought processes.

 ## THE ABSENT AUNT

Sam's mother asked him to drive down to the airport to meet his Aunt Janice who was arriving from Sydney, Australia. Sam's mother and Janice had been separated at birth, but had recently got in touch with each other. Never having seen his aunt before, Sam was worried that he might not recognize her, but his mother assured him that he wouldn't have a problem. How did she know? Sam hadn't seen a photo of Janice and she hadn't seen one of him. His mother hadn't seen her sister since infancy, so how did she expect Sam to recognize her?

◉ Answer on page 122.

 ## DEATH OF THE DEALER

In a speakeasy somewhere in Chicago during the 1930s, a group of mafiosi were playing poker. Some of them had been losing quite heavily and were not happy about it. Eventually one of them eyed the dealer narrowly and snarled, 'I say you're cheating!' This was unwise, to say the least. The dealer whipped out a snub-nosed Colt .45 and shot the player stone dead. The cops were called. The lieutenant in charge was a tough cookie and no slouch with a gun but, even though he was heavily armed and backed up by a deputy, he couldn't arrest any of the men present. Why not? There was no shortage of witnesses and the dealer didn't even deny what had happened.

◉ Answer on page 122.

 ## LAST SUPPER

Angela had been searching for Mickey and was devastated when she found him lying dead. He had clearly been eating a meal when he died, and an iron bar lay across his back. What had happened to him?

◉ Answer on page 122.

ODD ANIMALS

The following animals have something in common. Can you work out what it is?

- Koala bear
- Prairie dog
- Guinea pig
- Silkworm
- Firefly
- Bombay duck

- Answer on page 122.

SEA STORY

A certain vessel undertook an epic journey, and then arrived at a sea with no water. Even so, it was able to enter the sea and complete its journey. When the crew had completed their business, they were able to return home without difficulty. Can you name the vessel and the sea it entered?

- Answer on page 122.

SUCCESSFUL PLAYERS

Five men went to a large casino in Las Vegas. They played from 9 a.m. until 3 p.m. All were professional players. They didn't stop for any breaks, nobody left and nobody joined them. They played together all day and, by the time they finished, they all had more money than when they started. How is that possible?

- Answer on page 122.

POLITICAL PROBLEMS

From time to time, we all fantasize about showing politicians exactly what we think of them. One man took this desire to extremes by throwing tomatoes at his local representative. He was delighted when he achieved a direct hit, but then appalled when the politician dropped dead. Why did the man die from being hit by tomatoes?

- Answer on page 122.

PUZZLES TO TEST YOUR CREATIVE THOUGHT PROCESSES

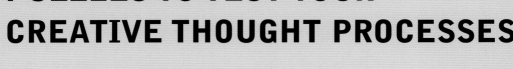

THREE SHORT PLANKS

Here are two puzzles that will test your ability to think originally. At first sight, the two tasks appear to be impossible but, with a little creative thought, they can be accomplished easily. As with so many creative solutions, the simplicity of the answer is breathtaking.

TASK 1
Circles A, B and C represent three islands. There is a man on each island. Each man has a short wooden plank that is not quite long enough to reach any of the other islands. How do the men form a bridge so that they may pass freely between the islands?

TASK 2
Now there are only two men, who are both on island A and have all three planks with them. How does one man get to island B and the other to island C?

⊙ Answer on page 122.

DOTTY DILEMMA

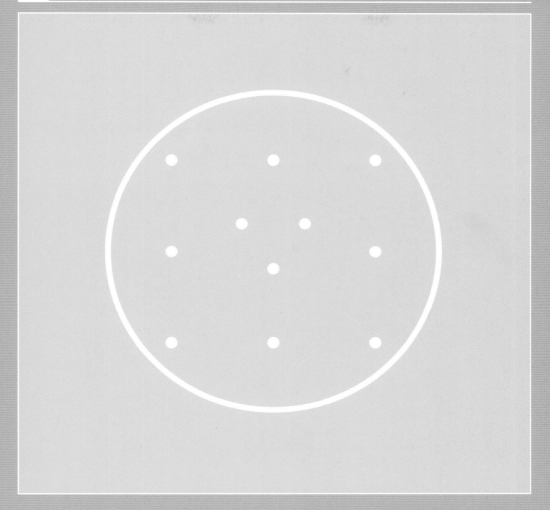

This is another chance to use your visual reasoning power. All you have to do is divide up the diagram by using four straight lines to form sectors containing one dot each. This is one of those puzzles that looks easy to begin with, then seems much more difficult than you thought. Finally, light dawns and the answer becomes obvious. If you can't do the puzzle straight away, please don't give up and look at the answers. Keep thinking! Go back to it again and again. There are no prizes for a quick solution. You will find that after a while, your unconscious mind will get to work on the problem and the solution will suddenly rise to the surface. This only happens if you first rack your brain to try to find the solution.

⊙ Answer on page 122.

THE VANISHING SQUARE

Matchstick puzzles are old favourites, but this one is a little bit special. You start out with sixteen matches forming five squares as shown.

All you have to do is move two matches to make a total of four squares instead of five, all of which must be the same size as the original ones.

How do you make a square vanish without having matches left over?

You can fiddle with this puzzle for ages before you find the solution. Do keep at it. The whole purpose of this section is to encourage you to have flashes of creative insight. The answer is not nearly as important as the process that helps you arrive at it.

◉ Answer on page 122.

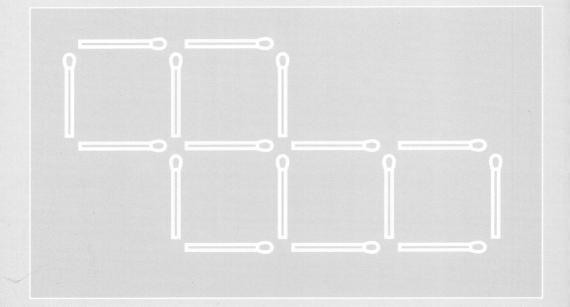

 ## WINE WOBBLE

For this task, take a wine glass, fill it with water and place it in a position where it cannot be picked up without causing all the water to be spilt. This last condition is very important. Most people who pick up a full glass will spill just a little liquid; the challenge in this case is to find a method that guarantees all the water is spilt.

◉ Answer on page 122.

MATCH PLAY

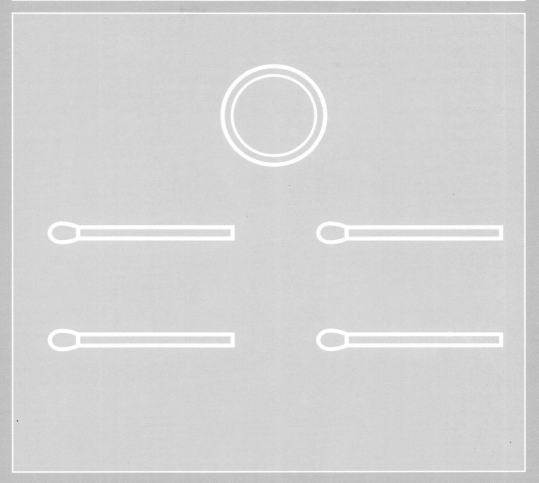

I like puzzles that require you to make a leap of imagination to reach the solution. This one is just such a puzzle. You need four matches and a cork. All you have to do is place the items on a table in such a way that the heads of the matches do not touch the cork or the table. The cork mustn't touch the table either.

◉ Answer on page 122.

THE HOLE STORY

A man went to an auction and saw an antique table. Unfortunately, it had a large and unsightly hole right in the middle. The man could never resist a bargain, however, so he bought the table and had it delivered to his house.

His family laughed, but the man had a cunning plan. Making a minimal number of cuts, he would saw up the table and join it together again, eliminating the hole and making a continuous surface.

When he had done this he was left with a beautiful piece of furniture.

How did the man cut the table and what did it look like when he had finished?

Here is a chance to come up with a really imaginative solution. Of course, all the man would have to do is make two long cuts to take out the middle chunk of the table and then just stick the two halves together again, but remember that the idea is to waste as little of the original wood as possible.

⊚ Answer on page 123.

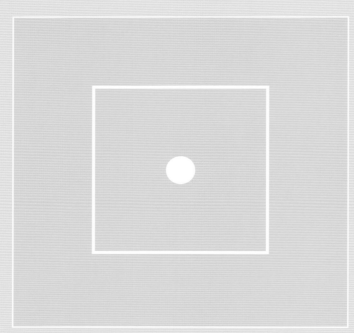

THE PUZZLING PRINCESS

The beautiful Princess Yasmin was captured by a ferocious genie, who carried her off to his lair. Because he enjoyed tormenting his captives he said to her, 'You can make a single statement. If it's true I will eat you, but if it's false I will feed you to my pet vultures.'

The plucky princess thought for a while and then made her statement. It was a very cunning one. The genie was so enraged that he exploded on the spot, and the princess escaped. What did she say?

⊚ Answer on page 123.

MAZE MYSTERY

This diagram shows the layout of the maze at the royal palace of Hampton Court in London. Finding your way to the centre of the maze is not that difficult if you're able to look at the whole thing from above, but it is much harder on the ground. Your task is to come up with a simple trick that will allow you to navigate the maze without any chance of getting lost.

⦿ Answer on page 123.

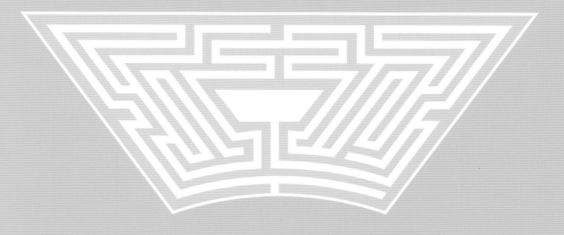

 WHICH LIST?

Here are two sets of words.

A	B
ARMY	RICE
YAM	WANDER
IDEAL	EVENTS
HURT	EEL
SAIL	LYRIC

Now decide whether the word 'YACHT' goes with list A or list B.

⦿ Answer on page 123.

NO WAY BACK

Here is one of those 'looks-simple-until-you-try-it' puzzles. What you have to do is reproduce the diagram on the right. There are, of course, a few rules:

- You must not cross any line.
- You must not retrace a line.
- You must not lift your pencil from the paper.

- Answer on page 123.

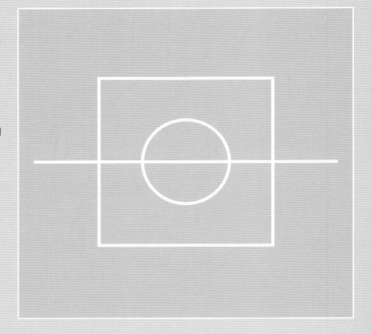

 ## ORIGINAL ORIGAMI

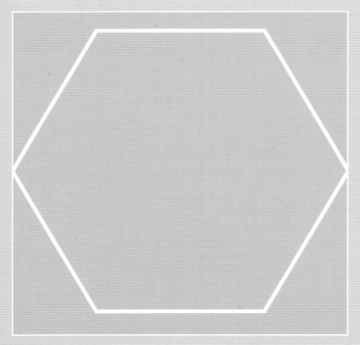

This time, your task is to fold a square sheet of paper and produce creases that form a hexagon. You aren't allowed to use pencils, rulers, protractors or any other tools. The whole thing can be accomplished simply by folding the paper. There are not many accurate folds that you can make freehand, so that gives you a good clue as to how to start. The rest is up to you.

- Answer on page 123.

DIVIDING THE DISC

It's very easy indeed to divide a disc into three equal parts with three lines, as illustrated here. But could you divide it into four equal parts using three lines of equal length? The lines don't have to be straight, and they mustn't cross. There is a simple, elegant solution to this puzzle. (Don't look too long at the disc illustrated: it will only set you thinking in the wrong direction.)

◉ Answer on page 123.

SHELL SHOCK

Hard-boil an egg and remove half the shell intact. Find a knife with a pointed blade. Hold the knife vertically, with the blade upwards, and pop the half-eggshell on to the tip of the knife. Now, rap the handle of the knife smartly on a tabletop, with the aim of getting the blade to pierce the eggshell.

You'll find this difficult, but see if you can discover the trick of it. Like all these puzzles, it takes just a little bit of extra thought.

Alternatively, if you are the practical type, you can just keep trying until you get it right by accident. All you then have to do is work out why that attempt was successful when all the others were not.

◉ Answer on page 123.

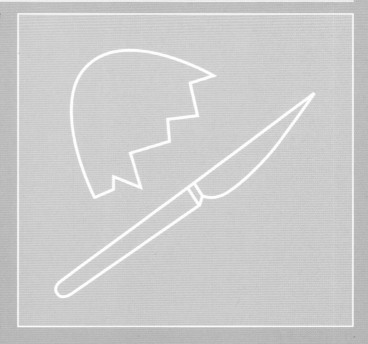

COIN CONUNDRUM

This puzzle starts with four rows of three coins, as illustrated.

Take the twelve coins and rearrange them into six rows of four coins each. This is another of those puzzles where the original diagram acts as a distraction and encourages you to think along conventional lines. Ignore it! The solution requires, as ever, a little spark of originality.

⊙ Answer on page 123.

 ## TOO MANY SQUARES

Take a square and divide it into eight rows of eight squares, as shown in diagram A. How many small squares are there? No, that's not the puzzle, that is just the easy bit – obviously there are sixty-four small squares. But now cut the square along the lines shown in the diagram and reassemble it to make the rectangle shown in diagram B. Now count the small squares. You'll find you have sixty-five small squares (five rows of thirteen)! The puzzle is to discover where the extra square came from.

⊙ Answer on page 123.

HUMILIATION!

This puzzle is not called 'Humiliation' for nothing. It has defeated people who are proud of their mathematical ability. As with so many problems, the temptation is to go looking for clever, complicated answers. The real answer is blindingly simple: if you wish to avoid humiliation, don't show this puzzle to your kids!

All you have to do is crack the logic of the puzzle and complete the final line.

◉ Answer on page 123.

1									
1	1								
2	1								
1	2	1	1						
1	1	1	2	2	1				
3	1	2	2	1	1				
1	3	1	1	2	2	2	1		
1	1	1	3	2	1	3	2	1	1
?	?	?	?	?	?	?	?	?	?

 ## CENTURY CONUNDRUM

The challenge here is to find a way of drawing the figure shown, without ever lifting your pencil from the paper. It looks impossible, but think about it for a while and you may just find you have a brainwave.

◉ Answer on page 124.

BERMUDA TRIANGLES

The Bermuda triangles puzzle is challenging because it subtly evolves as it goes along. Just as you think you've got the hang of it, you find that the puzzle has changed.

Because all the versions of the puzzle look very similar, it is easy to be misled into thinking they are all to be solved in the same way. Stay alert and look at each puzzle with fresh eyes. You may well find it difficult to follow this advice: you have been warned!

In each puzzle your task is the same: find a number or letter that logically replaces the question mark.

PUZZLE 1

This is a very simple example just to get you started. A bright eight-year-old could find the answer in seconds.

⊙ Answer on page 124.

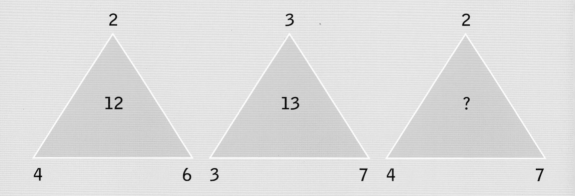

PUZZLE 2

Now try something a little more challenging. It is still a matter of finding a simple formula. A few tries should be all you need to work out how it is done.

⊙ Answer on page 124.

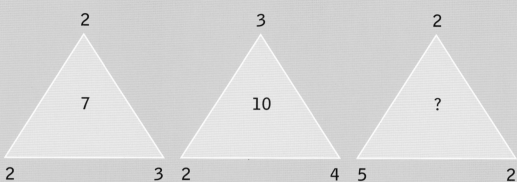

 PUZZLE 3

The formula has changed yet again. Can you work it out?

⊙ Answer on page 124.

 PUZZLE 4

Right, now it starts to get difficult. The maths is still childishly simple, but a complication has been introduced. Is your thinking flexible enough to work out what's going on?

⊙ Answer on page 124.

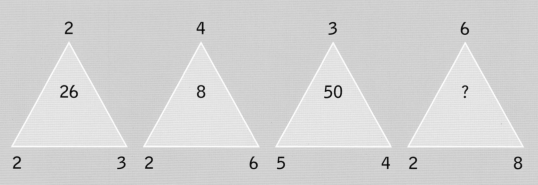

PUZZLE 5

Now a new trick has been introduced. Are you able to keep up? ⊙ Answer on page 124.

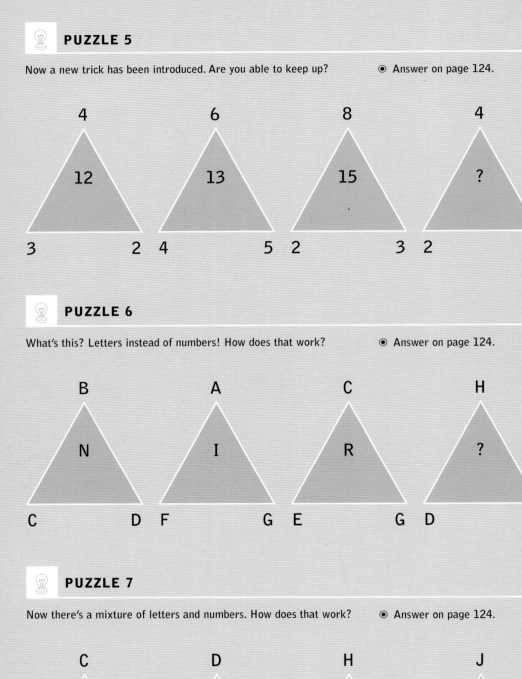

PUZZLE 6

What's this? Letters instead of numbers! How does that work? ⊙ Answer on page 124.

PUZZLE 7

Now there's a mixture of letters and numbers. How does that work? ⊙ Answer on page 124.

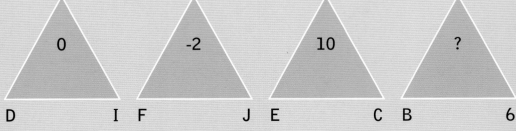

PUZZLE 8

By now you have probably got the hang of these puzzles, so this one won't cause you any problems at all.

⊙ Answer on page 124.

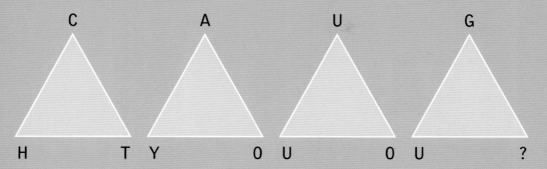

HOW DID YOU DO?

So, just how many of the answers did you get right?

All eight

Brilliant! If you managed to follow all the twists and turns as the puzzles changed their nature, it shows that your mental agility is of the highest order. You are clearly a creative thinker.

Five to seven

This is a pretty good score. You have managed to adapt your thinking to most of the changes called for, but your mental agility could be improved still further. The trick is never to assume that just because problems resemble each other superficially, they are going to be solved in the same way.

Three to four

You need to work quite hard on your problem-solving skills. Bear in mind that there is nothing really difficult about any of these puzzles. Your defeat is not because of a lack of mathematical ability, but purely down to a lack of imagination.

One to two

This is a poor result. You are far too inflexible in your thinking. When faced with problems like these, you need to come up with as many theories as possible. If you are sufficiently prolific, you will find that eventually you hit on the right idea.

TRANSPLANTATION

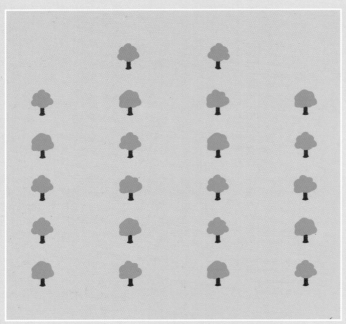

Here is a cunning little problem that will take a bit of sorting out. The picture shows an orchard of twenty-two trees. The owner wants to form twenty rows of four trees by transplanting six of the trees.

⊙ Answer on page 124.

PAPER PUZZLE

This seems like an impossible task – for the very good reason that it is – until you think of a very simple trick that will solve your problem.

Take a strip of paper about 2.5 cm (1 in) wide and 1 m (39 in) in length. Now, the task is to get a pencil and draw a line down the centre of the strip, on both sides of the paper at once. This really is much easier than it sounds.

⊙ Answer on page 124.

CASH PROBLEM

Take five coins and arrange them so that each coin is touching every other coin. This is one of those problems that can take ages to solve, but then, with a sudden leap of imagination, it all becomes clear. On the other hand, some people see the solution at a glance.

⊙ Answer on page 124.

DEAD END

This picture is taken from an actual gravestone in Monmouth, where a man named John Renie is buried. The inscription reads 'Here lies John Renie'. If you move from letter to contiguous letter (including diagonals), how many times is the inscription written? This puzzle will not do much for your creative powers, but it is a wonderful aid to concentration.

◉ Answer on page 124.

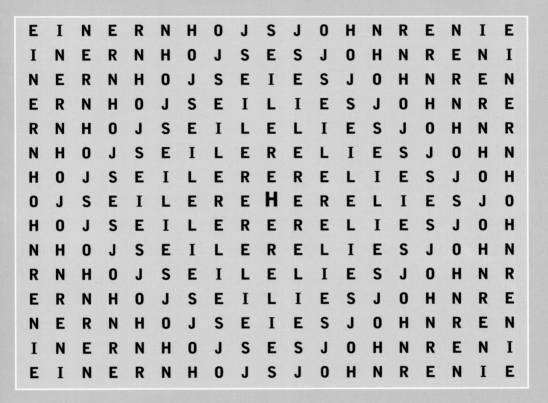

MATCH MYSTERY

The diagram shows seven matches arranged to represent a fraction – one-seventh – and written in Roman numerals. Your task is to rearrange the matches to make one-third. You must use all the matches. What's creative about this? Well, there is more than one answer to the problem so, when you've found one solution, see if you can find any others.

◉ Answer on page 124.

TRIANGLE TOTALS

Take a triangle like the one shown.

Now take the digits 1, 2, 3, 4, 5, 6, 7, 8, 9 and place them at the vertices and along the sides of the triangle so that the numbers on each side add up to twenty. It isn't easy, but you will be glad to hear that there is more than one way of doing it.

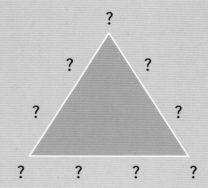

⊚ Answer on page 124.

 ## CUP CONUNDRUM

The nice thing about this puzzle is that once you have the answer, you can try it out on other innocent victims.

Take an ordinary teacup, a length of string and a pair of scissors. Tie the teacup to a door handle with the string. Then, with the scissors, cut the string in two places without letting the cup fall to the ground. Like all puzzles of this sort, it appears difficult until you know the answer!

⊚ Answer on page 125.

 ## CHAIR CHALLENGE

Sam went to a dance, but he was out of luck because none of the girls would be his partner. While sitting rather miserably, hoping that his luck would change, he started looking at his surroundings. He noticed that there were ten chairs in the room and, being a bit of a geek at heart, he started to work out how to arrange the chairs so that there would be three on each side of the room. How did he do it?

⊚ Answer on page 125.

 ## HANKY PANKY

You are given a glass tumbler and a handkerchief. Your mission is to push the handkerchief into the glass and then immerse it in a bowl of water without getting the cloth wet.

⊚ Answer on page 125.

QUILT QUESTION

This is a stiff test of your ingenuity. You have twenty pieces of silk, all of the same triangular shape and size. You discover that four of them will fit together to form a perfect square, as in the illustration. How do you fit all twenty together to form a perfectly square patchwork cushion? There must be no waste (and no allowance need be made for hems).

◉ Answer on page 125.

 JUMBLED LETTERS

Rearrange the following letters to form just one word.

◉ Answer on page 125.

D	E	J	N	O	O	R	S	T	U	W

A TORRENT OF IDEAS

Human ingenuity is such that ideas pour from our minds all the time, in a great flood. Not all these ideas, however, are of equal value. Some will undoubtedly be brilliant, others will be useful but not world-shattering, some will be of only minor interest and the huge majority will be either useless or plain crazy.

The trick – and it's a very difficult trick – is to separate one from the other. Many ideas that initially appeared crazy and impossible were later acclaimed as huge advances in civilization.

The history of civilization has been a constant struggle between those who produce new ideas and those who try to suppress them. The battle has always been fiercely fought and still is. It is easy, with the benefit of hindsight, to view someone like Galileo as a great scientist who was cruelly persecuted by the bigots of the Roman Inquisition. But new ideas are always met with similar resistance. There are very few innovative thinkers who have not been accused of being stupid, mad, evil or just plain wrong-headed. Only very persistent people, and very good ideas, survive the forces of reaction that are ranged against them. Does this mean that the world has been deprived of many wonderful ideas that were crushed by the criticism of bigots? Or does it mean that we have been saved from a great many dangerous notions by people who saw the potential risks? We will, of course, never know. But what we do know is

DANGEROUS THINKING

Galileo had the wild and dangerous notion that the earth orbits the Sun. He wrote:

I hold that the Sun is located at the centre of the revolutions of the heavenly orbs and does not change place, and that the Earth rotates on itself and moves around it. Moreover ... I confirm this view not only by refuting Ptolemy's and Aristotle's arguments, but also by producing many for the other side, especially some pertaining to physical effects whose causes perhaps cannot be determined in any other way, and other astronomical discoveries; these discoveries clearly confute the Ptolemaic system, and they agree admirably with this other position and confirm it.

ONLY A FEW IDEAS SUCCEED

Edison is known for major inventions, such as the electric light bulb and the phonograph. In fact, he produced some 1,300 inventions, many of which never saw the light of day. This is Edison's electric pen. The idea was that a needle, powered by a Bunsen battery (the two glass jars), would vibrate and make small holes in a sheet of stiff paper. The sheet was then to be used as a stencil from which thousands of copies could be made. Like many bright ideas, it was never popular because even better ways were found to do the job.

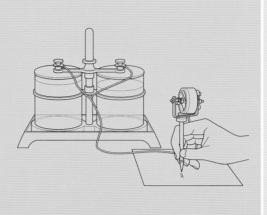

that, in order to survive and prosper, a new idea must be very good indeed. Once you do have a good idea and it starts to circulate, it has tremendous power and will be all but impossible to combat.

In this section we will look at a number of areas of human activity and the way in which new ideas have struggled for recognition. Ideas thrust their way into our consciousness all the time, although many are cut down before they are fully formed. Even people who are noted for their bright ideas, such as Thomas Edison, have quite a low success rate (see box above).

AN ECCENTRIC GENIUS

Isaac Newton, a mathematical genius who laid down much of the foundation of modern physics, never lost his interest in alchemy – the 'science' of turning base metals into gold. After his death, his friends were mortified to discover a number of manuscripts that not only described alchemical theories, but also contained strange prophecies about the end of the world, based on his interpretation of the Book of Daniel in the Bible. It seems that genius is no bar to having eccentric ideas.

IT STANDS TO REASON

In every age, including our own, there have been received ideas that, for most people, are simply self-evident – they are said to 'stand to reason'. Such ideas are often wildly wrong, but that is no bar to them being believed.

It is easy to look back over history and smile at the things that many people thought were perfectly reasonable. At one time, the idea that the world is flat was seen as an incontrovertible truth. Nowadays, most people consider this idea to be patently absurd (although there are still groups who maintain that it is true).

LOUIS PASTEUR

We could easily fill a whole book with ideas that were once held to be common sense but are no longer believed. Another book could be written about the innovative ideas that were loudly denounced as being crazy or fraudulent. Let's just limit ourselves to a couple of instructive examples. First, we might look at the assertion by Louis Pasteur that the world is teeming with microbes and that some of these are the source of the illnesses suffered by humans and animals. One of the popular arguments used to rebut this theory was that if the air were full of micro-organisms, these would blot out all the light and people would not be able to see. Anyone who has ever seen dust motes illuminated by a beam of sunlight knows that the atmosphere teems with all sorts of matter – you do not need complicated scientific equipment to see this phenomenon. Yet Pasteur's critics were able to rely on this twaddle as a supposedly serious objection to his ideas. This vividly demonstrates that a new idea is often not just met with benign scepticism or constructive criticism, but with a sort of blind hatred that will use any sort of perverted reasoning in an attempt to discredit it.

ORVILLE AND WILBUR WRIGHT

An even more famous example of this phenomenon is the reception given to the Wright brothers. On 17 December 1903, at Kitty Hawk, North Carolina, Orville Wright made the first powered aeroplane flight in history. Even though there were five witnesses, this achievement was met with complete apathy on the part of the newspapers. As late as 1905, *Scientific American* magazine condemned the report of the Wrights' success as a hoax. In that same year, however, the brothers made a half-hour flight of 38 km (24 miles). It was not until 1908, when they flew in Le Mans, France, that their achievement was universally recognized.

Acceptance of the Wrights' aeronautical feat did not depend on understanding some complex scientific theory. They flew repeatedly, and the evidence was available for anyone with a pair of eyes. However, since the scientific establishment (and those who understood the science involved) 'knew' that such a flight was impossible, no one was prepared to waste their time going to see the efforts of a couple of obvious tricksters.

THE PHILOSOPHERS' STONE

The importance of being able to replicate an experiment is impossible to overemphasize, but it may be illustrated by the unfortunate fate of James Price, a Fellow of the Royal Society in London. In 1783 Price claimed to have found the alchemists' goal, the philosophers' stone (a substance thought to change base metals into gold). He tried to repeat his experiment in front of other scientists but failed. Then, to the astonishment of the witnesses, he drank prussic acid and died on the spot.

PUTTING A NEW IDEA TO THE TEST

In theory, science offers a fair method of evaluating new ideas. The basic scientific method goes like this:

⊙ Scientists analyse measured data.

⊙ Scientists formulate theories that fit the data.

⊙ Scientists perform experiments designed to disprove the theories.

⊙ If those experiments fail to disprove the theories, the theories gain weight.

⊙ The most important rule for designing experiments is that they must be replicable by another experimenter.

⊙ There is an important distinction between failing to disprove a theory and proving a theory. It is impossible to prove a scientific theory.

⊙ All results are published and made available for peer review. In other words, scientists have to be able to convince other scientists in the field that their results are valid.

This process should ensure that new ideas are given a fair hearing and accepted or rejected on purely objective grounds. Sadly, this is a long way from being the truth. In fact, scientists have been as willing as anybody else to let prejudice and bigotry influence their views.

THE WRIGHT BROTHERS offered their invention to the US War Department but were dismissed as cranks.

It should be apparent, even from this very brief look at the subject, that original thinking in science and technology is a hazardous business. This is an area where people pride themselves on being at their most logical and objective but, as we have seen, this is very far from the truth.

THE BEE DANCE

Honeybees regularly face a rather tricky problem – of how to tell other bees where food is located. Imagine that it is spring, the food supply in the hive has run down during the winter and one bee flies off to scout for food. It finds a field full of flowering clover – a huge larder that could keep the whole hive well fed for ages. How does it tell the others where to go? In the early 1900s, Austrian naturalist Karl von Frisch tackled this problem and discovered that the bees perform dances to convey to other bees exactly where food is located. Different dances, coupled with sounds, can convey the distance, direction, quality and quantity of a food supply. For example, the 'round dance' indicates that the nectar is less than 32 m (104 ft) away. The scout bee performs circles to the left and the right; the richer the food source, the longer and more vigorous the dance. The so-called 'waggle dance' tells other bees that the food is more than 32 m (104 ft) away. The scout bee makes two loops, with a straight run in the middle. The direction of the straight run shows where food can be found.

Needless to say, von Frisch's theory was regarded as utter nonsense by most scientists of the time. The idea that animals, let alone insects, were capable of complex communication drove many researchers to the brink of apoplexy. Over time, however, the theory of the bee dance not only gained acceptance but, because it is a rather nice, quirky idea, it became well known to people outside the scientific community. Nowadays the bee dance is part of orthodox thought, even though many scientists still have very serious problems with it.

Even more interestingly, Creationists (those who believe that the world was specially created by God, and did not evolve in the way Darwin described) have seized on the bee dance as a way supporting their world view. They ask how the bee could have taught the meaning of its dance to the other bees. How could it tell them that if it wiggles

CREATIVITY TIP

Always look for new experiences that will stretch your mind. For example, listen to new music, read a magazine that you don't normally look at, watch a TV documentary on a subject you know nothing about, go somewhere new, talk to new people. If you always stick to your usual routine, you make it hard for new things to influence and inspire you.

very slowly it means the field is very distant, and if it waggles very fast it means the field is not as far away? How would they know that if the dancer walks up the honeycomb they should fly towards the sun, but if the bee walks down they must fly in the opposite direction? Also, if this process evolved over a long time, how would all the bee ancestors have survived while this system of communication was evolving? If they survived without this complicated method, why invent a new system that would be almost impossible to explain?

A SUCCESSFUL EXPERIMENT

Francis Bacon was one of the first men of science to insist that theories should be tested by practical experiment. On a winter's day in 1626, at the age of sixty-five, he was travelling by coach up London's Highgate Hill in the company of his friend Dr Witherborne. The two men were discussing how food could be preserved by ice. It was a snowy day and so Bacon proposed an experiment. He bought a chicken and got the vendor to kill and gut it. Then Bacon stuffed the carcass with snow. Unfortunately, he got so cold while all this was going on that he became ill and had to be taken to the nearby house of his friend, the Earl of Arundel. His illness got worse and on 19 April he died. However, he wrote this in his last letter: 'As for the experiment itself, it succeeded excellently well.'

TAMING A WILD IDEA

A few years ago, I was involved in a project to set up a website for selling wine. This was at the height of the dotcom boom, when everyone thought they could become internet millionaires.

In spite of our heady optimism, we were well aware that there were already many wine sites, several of them run by large, wealthy companies that had the advantage of being able to buy wine in huge quantities and therefore at rock-bottom prices. Our challenge was to find a way in which a small company, with only slender means, could find a niche in the market. The project involved four people: a wine expert, a computer 'techie', a business expert and me. Our first step was to have a brainstorming session. We met in one of those cafés that has paper tablecloths, and scribbled all our ideas on the paper. The illustration below is a reconstruction of what the tablecloth looked like by the time we had finished.

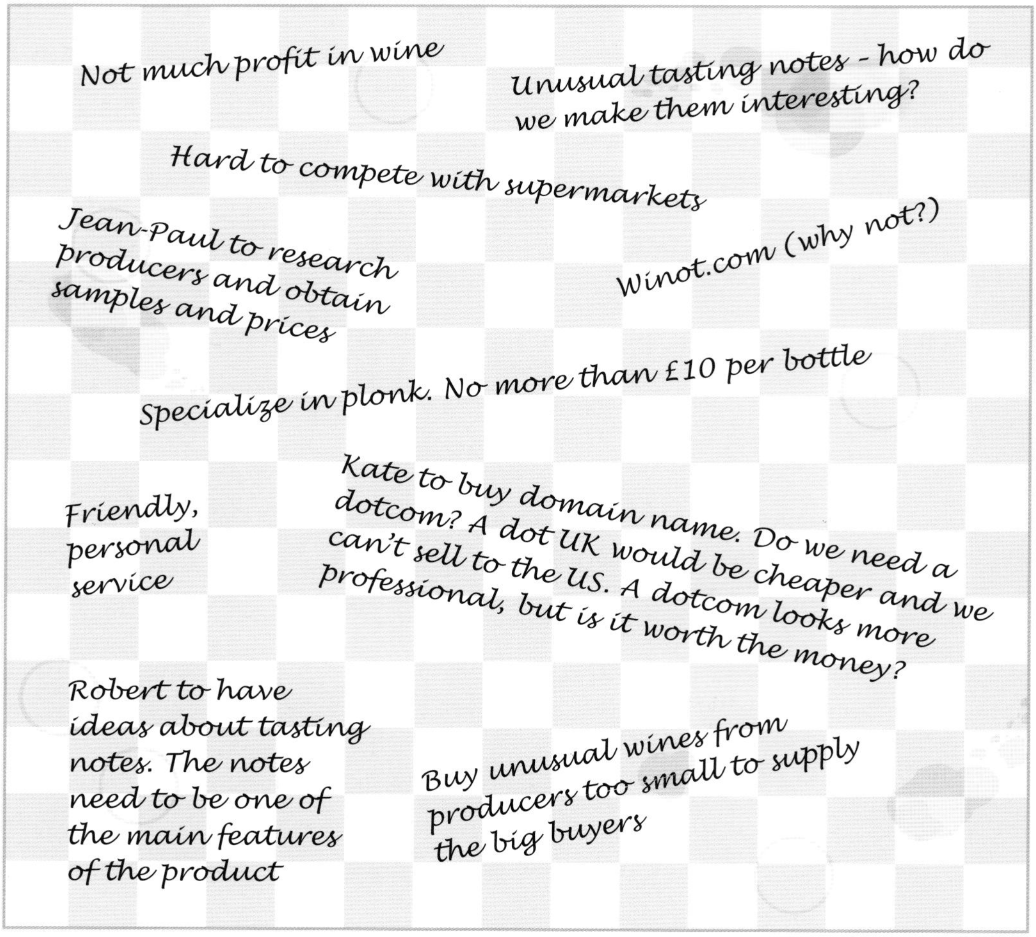

Not much profit in wine

Unusual tasting notes – how do we make them interesting?

Hard to compete with supermarkets

Jean-Paul to research producers and obtain samples and prices

Winot.com (why not?)

Specialize in plonk. No more than £10 per bottle

Friendly, personal service

Kate to buy domain name. Do we need a dotcom? A dot UK would be cheaper and we can't sell to the US. A dotcom looks more professional, but is it worth the money?

Robert to have ideas about tasting notes. The notes need to be one of the main features of the product

Buy unusual wines from producers too small to supply the big buyers

AFTER THE STORM

This has all the hallmarks of a good brainstorming session. You can see that the discussion was lively and produced a good crop of ideas. The people involved are not part of any corporate structure, all have an equal share in the venture and all are happy to share their thoughts with few inhibitions. As you would expect at this early stage, the ideas are still quite random and nothing has been thought through properly. However, certain themes are developing. There is already a consensus about the sort of wine we want to sell and the intended customers. People have already taken on particular responsibilities, and will go away from the meeting with certain tasks to undertake and ideas to explore. One of the group undertook to take the tablecloth of notes home and type them out in full. We agreed that there should be no editing at this stage – all we wanted was a complete list of all the comments that had been made. Before the next meeting the comments were e-mailed to all the participants, and a number of one-to-one discussions took place.

The second meeting was held in the same café and used up another paper tablecloth. This time, however, it was possible to produce some order out of the chaos. The illustration of the second tablecloth shows how the initial brainstorming of ideas has matured into a cogent business plan.

Kate has managed to buy Winot.com.

The site will only carry unusual wines from small producers who are happy to sell in small quantities.

Jean-Paul has visited some producers and brought back samples. We will have a tasting on Thursday evening.

Some people at Deutschebank have heard about the site and would like a wine-tasting party.

PERPETUAL MOTION

One crazy notion that has persisted over the years is that it is possible to design a machine that, once it has been set in motion, will keep on working in perpetuity.

According to the best scientific advice available, such a machine is an impossibility because it would violate any number of natural laws. This has in no way deterred people from trying to design such a device. In fact, even now the US Patent Office has felt it necessary to offer the following advice to those who wish to register a patent.

The views of the Patent Office are in accord with those scientists who have investigated the subject and are to the effect that such devices are physical impossibilities. The position of the Office can only be rebutted by a working model. The Office hesitates to accept fees from applicants who believe they have discovered perpetual motion, and deems it only fair to give such applicants a word of warning that fees cannot be recovered after the case has been considered by the Examiner.

This is a perfect illustration of the way in which people will constantly seek to innovate even when they are given really serious discouragement. The feeling seems to be, 'Oh, so it's impossible, eh? OK, that's all the more reason for me to do it.' Those who are determined to produce a perpetual motion machine, in spite of warnings that it is impossible, will, of course, quite rightly point out that many things once thought to be impossible have since been done. This is one of the great charms of creativity. It spurs people on to attempt great things by showing them, from time to time, that what was thought to be beyond our reach can, in fact, be achieved.

NOW TRY THIS

As an exercise in creativity, try to design your own perpetual motion machine. It can be quite an interesting challenge to come up with a machine that works in theory, and it will stimulate your creative spirit. And, of course, there is always just that outside chance that the scientists are wrong and your machine will actually work. In any case, if you don't try, you'll never know…

CREATIVE TIP

It is often a good idea to spend some time visualizing what you think a project will look like when it's finished. This can sometimes show you the path from where you are now to where you will be at the end.

DESIGNS THAT TRIED AND FAILED

Here is an ingenious design for a perpetual motion machine. Like all such inventions it appears at first sight to be a clever idea but, once built, it simply won't work. The self-blowing windmill was produced by an Italian named Marco Zimara in the early 1500s. A gust of wind would turn the sails which in turn would operate a bellows that produced enough wind to keep the sails turning. The machine didn't work because the force needed to work the bellows was more than the windmill could produce. The idea of perpetual motion has fascinated inventors for centuries. Nowadays anyone who knows anything about science understands that the idea violates a number of natural laws. Has that stopped people trying? Not at all. There are still people who labour valiantly, reminding themselves that history is littered with examples of the 'impossible' which eventually became possible. And who is to say they are wrong? Once a human being gets that gleam of creativity in the eye there is no knowing what will happen next.

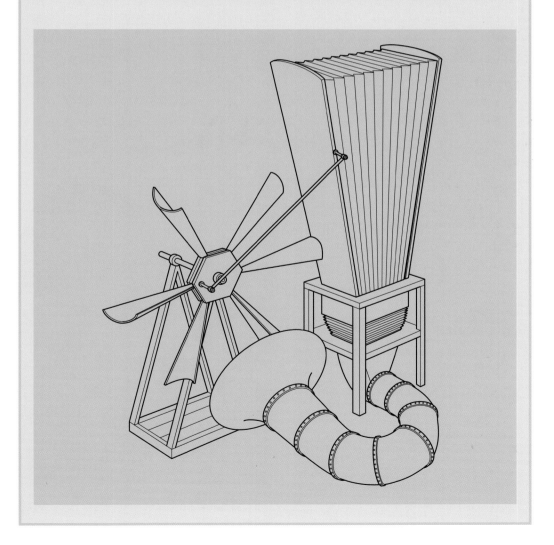

HARNESSING THE POWER OF THE TWILIGHT ZONE

Maddeningly, creativity does not reside in the conscious part of the mind, where we can access it readily, but in the unconscious part, over which we have little, if any, control.

Beneath the thin crust of rationality lies a great ocean of ideas that, if we're lucky, will sometimes pop into consciousness to illuminate our rather dreary thought processes. So do you just have to sit around waiting for inspiration? Certainly not! In fact that is the very worst thing you can do. Inspiration is rather like lightning, – in that although you certainly can't control it, you can encourage it to strike. Remember Benjamin Franklin? When he wanted to study lightning, he famously flew a kite bearing a large metal key into a thunderstorm – dangerous but effective! You needn't do anything that risky. In fact, our first technique for awaking the unconscious is decidedly restful.

DALI'S DEVICE

The Spanish surrealist Salvador Dali noticed that he would get amazing, outlandish ideas just as he was on the verge of sleep; however, when he woke up they'd be gone and no matter how hard he tried, he couldn't remember them. Here's how he overcame the problem (you can try this at home).

He sat down in a comfortable armchair, ready to take a nap. On the floor beside him, he placed a metal plate, and in his hand he held a spoon. As he nodded off, his grip on the spoon would loosen and the resultant clatter as it fell on the plate would wake him up. Being woken right in the middle of the so-called 'twilight zone' would allow him to access the ideas that had proved so elusive before. Try the simple techniques opposite to access the power of your twilight zone.

ARTIST SALVADOR DALI arrives in New York with a rooster whose acquaintance he made on his trip.

Continued from page 26

Did you say 'carrot'? When tested, 98% of people give the same answer. This isn't magic (though at first you might think it is); instead it is a perfect example of how, quite unwittingly, we tend to think in boxes. The moral of this tale is: beware the box – especially the one you don't know you're in.

BEAUTIFUL DREAMER

The first technique exploits our ability to have lucid dreams. When you dream, it is not uncommon to find that you have superhuman powers. Most of us remember dreams where we have been able to fly, speak foreign languages or fight off monsters with ease. But suppose you could actually control your dream? Suppose you could harness those powers and use them at will? Impossible? A growing number of people believe that it is not only possible, but fairly simple. How do you do it?

⦿ Start by taking note of your dreams.

⦿ Make a regular effort to recall dreams in detail, writing them down if necessary (but not telling them to other people, which is a boring thing to do).

⦿ Once you have become familiar with your dream world, give yourself a code word or gesture with which to remind yourself that you are dreaming.

Once you have perfected the technique, you will be able to use your dream life to your advantage. Now you will be able to wander at will in the sea of the unconscious, and draw on whatever inspiration you find there.

⦿ Now for the tricky bit – you must try to condition yourself to become aware that you are dreaming and to use your coded word or gesture to confirm to yourself that, although in a dream state, you are now lucid. Some people find this quite easy, others require practice.

SLEEP ON IT

Did your mother ever encourage you to solve a problem by saying, 'Sleep on it, things always look better in the morning'? She had a point. While you sleep, your mind keeps on working and, humiliating though it is to admit, the mind often gets on much better without our (rational) interruptions. How does this help creativity? Try the following experiment.

⦿ Take a work problem to bed with you and go through the points carefully before you go to sleep. Don't just glance at a few papers, but really make an effort to wrestle with the problem and solve it by using your normal powers of reasoning. If you're really tired and find yourself thinking rubbish, so much the better! This is just the sort of state of mind you need to be in.

⦿ When you feel that you really can't go on any longer, it's time to turn in for the night.

⦿ If it's practicable, put your notebook (or some notes on a sheet of paper) under your pillow. This will ensure that the problem you're wrestling with will be high on the agenda when your subconscious kicks in after you fall asleep.

As soon as you wake, you're likely to find that you have several solutions to the problem. Write them down immediately!

SELF-HYPNOSIS

One way of reaching the twilight zone is to use self-hypnosis. This is a simple, but very effective technique that allows you to liberate your mind from the bonds that normally constrain it.

Hypnosis uses a state of deep relaxation to allow suggestions to be fed directly into the unconscious mind, without going through the usual process of comprehension and evaluation that the conscious mind applies to new information. It is possible to buy hypnotic tapes that promise to boost your creativity, but the problem with these is that they rely on allowing a disembodied voice to lull you into a hypnotic state and then whisper suggestions to you. Some people find it scary to allow a complete stranger such a degree of access to their mind. The alternative therefore is to do the job yourself. This is quite a simple technique that anyone can learn.

First, choose a time when you will be alone and undisturbed. You should practise your self-hypnosis at a regular time and not just whenever the fancy takes you. Make sure, as far as possible, that you are not going to be interrupted (for example, turn off your phone).

PHASE 1 – RELAXATION

- Sit or lie in a comfortable position. It is possible that you will fall asleep at some point, so make sure that the position you have chosen will allow you to do this safely.

- Close your eyes and start to breathe slowly and deeply. Focus all your attention on your breathing. Keep this up until you feel completely comfortable.

- Now, start relaxing all the muscles in your body. Begin with your feet. First, clench all the muscles tightly. Hold for a few seconds and then relax. Repeat the process. You will find that the process of tensing and then relaxing your muscles leaves them feeling completely relaxed.

- Move up to your calves and once again tense the muscles for a few seconds and then relax. Repeat this process.

- Slowly work your way up the body, tensing and relaxing each group of muscles as you go. The groups to work on are: feet, calves, thighs, buttocks, stomach, back, arms, hands, chest, neck, face and scalp. Make especially sure that you relax the muscles in your stomach, chest and face, as these are areas that are particularly prone to tension.

- Now your whole body should be completely relaxed. You are ready to enter the hypnotic state.

OTHER WAYS TO USE SELF-HYPNOSIS

The technique outlined above will, if used regularly, give your creative powers a boost. Once you are adept at inducing the hypnotic state, you can use it to tackle specific problems. For example, if you have reached a point in one of your projects where you don't know how to progress to the next phase, the tape can be adapted specifically to encourage you to find an answer to your problem. This is a very useful way of getting to grips with a creative block

PHASE 2 – INDUCING HYPNOSIS

In preparation for this phase, you should record a tape to listen to, containing instructions for deepening the hypnotic state. Talk in a quiet, calm voice and repeat each instruction several times. There are several things you need to include on the tape, as follows:

- Tell yourself to imagine that you are in a warm, safe, comfortable place. This can be anywhere you like. You can use a real place, or an imaginary one if that suits you better. The only requirement is that the place should give you a feeling of complete security.

- Now you are ready to deepen your hypnotic state. Do this by counting down slowly from a hundred. You will quite probably go to sleep during this phase (though it doesn't matter if you don't). Just keep listening to your own voice as it soothes and relaxes you.

- Now you are ready for the suggestions. These can be of any sort you like but, for present purposes, we will look at suggestions that will improve your creativity. It is very important that all the suggestions you use are positive and encouraging. Don't tell yourself not to do things. Concentrate on telling yourself that you are a creative and original person who has a constant supply of bright ideas. (If you want, visualize yourself fishing for bright ideas in an ocean. The ideas look like brightly coloured fish, and you have a net full of the ones you have already caught. Alternatively, you could visualize the creative urge flowing through you like a warm liquid that enters and soothes every part of your body.)

- Before you finish, you might choose to include a number of affirmations that will help boost the positive view of your creative abilities that you are trying to create. Here are some examples:

I am a channel for creativity.

I have well-developed creative talents.

My work is productive and fulfilling.

I feel the creative urge within me all the time.

I am always open to the flow of new ideas.

I am confident and competent in my creative work.

I am eager to experience my creative energy.

My life is rewarding and creative.

I am willing to think creatively.

- Finally, bring yourself gently out of the hypnotic state. Do this by counting backwards from ten to one. Pause during the count to tell yourself that you are waking up. When you get to the end of the count, tell yourself to wake up and open your eyes. It is important that waking up from the hypnotized state is done gently.

- Always have a pad and pen beside you so that you can jot down any good ideas that occurred to you while in the hypnotic state. Remember that such ideas are highly volatile and will evaporate within seconds of your waking, so it is important to catch them straight away.

DOES SELF-HYPNOSIS REALLY WORK?

I can give a personal example of this technique at work. I was phoned by one of my clients, a publisher who had just purchased a licence to turn the game of Scrabble into a book. There was just one small problem – he didn't know how it could be done. He asked me to go away and come up with some ideas. I played around with the problem for a while, but could not come up with anything that worked. Eventually, I decided to make this project the subject of a self-hypnosis session. Once I stopped thinking about the problem and allowed myself to relax into the hypnotic state, the solution came to me in a flash. I immediately jotted down a few notes and was able to use these to produce a proposal that was quickly accepted by the publisher.

UNCONSCIOUS INCUBATION

While Leonardo da Vinci was painting *The Last Supper* in the refectory of the Convent of Santa Maria delle Grazie, he frequently worked from dawn to dusk.

But from time to time, he would take a break and apparently spend time doing nothing. The prior, who was responsible for the work, was annoyed and repeatedly asked him to get on with the job and finish it. Leonardo was unmoved and so, eventually, the prior complained to the duke. When Leonardo was asked why he took so much time off from his work he replied, 'The greatest geniuses sometimes accomplish more when they work less.'

Clearly, Leonardo knew the value of 'unconscious incubation' – the process in which the unconscious mind keeps working on a problem while the conscious mind stops thinking about it. It is a humbling thought that the mind frequently works better without our interference. You have probably had the experience of wrestling with a problem without coming to a solution and then, after you have stopped thinking about it, the answer suddenly comes to you in a flash of inspiration. The unconscious mind is a great mystery. If it were merely a storehouse for all the things that we don't need to think about immediately, that would be quite understandable. But the unconscious is far more complex than that. It keeps thinking all the time, whether we are awake or asleep. From time to time, it throws up notions in a way that seems quite random. Certainly, it is outside our conscious control. The activities of the unconscious are many and varied. It can, for example, blind us to thoughts that we would rather not entertain. Alternatively, it can force such thoughts upon us and make us incapable of thinking about anything else. Sometimes it generates thoughts that seem to have no immediate relevance to anything. Are such thoughts truly random, or does the unconscious have some purpose of its own that the conscious mind can't penetrate?

WORKING ON A PROBLEM

This is not the place to go too deeply into the workings of the mind. Let us confine ourselves to ways in which 'unconscious incubation' can be used to help our creative

LEONARDO DA VINCI knew the importance of taking a break from work.

CREATIVE TRIGGERS

It is possible to make a trigger (such as a gesture) that you deliberately associate with creative thought. For example, you could run the tip of your index finger up and down the bridge of your nose whenever you are involved in creative thinking. When you have a bright idea, make sure that you use your trigger. Eventually, the process can be made to work the other way round, and the use of your gesture will prompt you to enter your creative mode and produce bright ideas.

powers. Although there is no sure way of making the unconscious work on a problem, there are things we can do to give it encouragement. Here are some of them:

- Spend as much time as you can attempting to work out the problem with your conscious mind. Use all your ingenuity to try to find a solution. It doesn't matter if all the ideas you come up with are no good. The important thing is to focus your mind upon the problem and to consider it from every angle.

- Write down all the possible solutions or, at the very least, make notes of the difficulties you encounter and the reasons that no solution has been found. It is very important to go through this phase of the operation as thoroughly as possible. The unconscious mind will not provide flashes of inspiration unless you have exhausted more conventional methods first.

- Now, take a break. It really doesn't matter what you do but it should be something that has no relation to your problem.

- Leave your problem alone for at least twenty-four hours. If no solution presents itself, go back to thinking consciously about possible solutions.

- With luck, one of two things will eventually happen. The unconscious may throw up a fully formed solution. Or, while you are working on the problem with your conscious mind, you will suddenly be able to work out what to do, whereas before you drew a blank.

- Because the unconscious is utterly unpredictable, there is no guarantee that a solution will be forthcoming at all. However, it sometimes happens that the problem will incubate for months or even years. This is why it is important always to keep a note of all your ideas. You just never know what is going to come to the surface.

THE ADVENTURES OF HUCKLEBERRY FINN

In the late summer of 1883, at Quarry Farm, in southern New York State, Mark Twain finally finished a book that, according to his own account, he had 'been fooling over for seven years'. This is a clear example of the way in which creative tasks cannot be hurried. Doubtless if Twain had tried to force the pace and finish his work quickly, it would have been a much lesser book than the one we now know – *The Adventures of Huckleberry Finn*. It took seven years of unconscious incubation before it was finally fully formed and ready to be published.

UNDER PRESSURE

So far, we have considered ways in which we can encourage creativity by relaxing and allowing ideas to flow in a rather unpredictable fashion.

This is a very popular view of the way creativity works, because relaxing is so agreeable. Unfortunately, the idea has taken hold that in order to be creative, all you have to do is sit around dreaming all day. If only this were true! The bad news is that for much of the time, people will want you to produce bright ideas in a hurry. The good news is that this pressure can be quite stimulating and often works in your favour. Sometimes when you simply have to produce an answer within a certain time you find that you can do it.

Some people thrive on this sort of pressure. In media careers such as journalism, broadcasting or advertising, working under pressure is quite normal. Often, if you are given a long time to complete a task, you find that instead of using the time to produce a beautiful and original piece of work, you either turn to more pressing matters and go back to the original task only when it has become urgent.

The puzzles that follow are deliberately designed to be stressful. You won't have nearly as much time as you would like to complete them. Even so, try to stick to the deadlines and surprise yourself with how much you can get done in the time available.

FIVE-MINUTE CHALLENGE

This is a little test to see how much you can accomplish when put under pressure of time. The three tasks below are not hard, but you have only five minutes to solve all of them.

BEHEADINGS

In each case you have to cut the first letter off a common word to produce another.

1. Behead a piece of furniture to get 'talented'.

2. Behead a structure to get 'everything'.

3. Behead a murmur to get 'an absolute'.

4. Behead violently thrown to get 'an organ of the body'.

5. Behead a light to get 'a speaker'.

6. Behead a weed to get 'a devotee'.

7. Behead a fruit to get 'variety'.

8. Behead a boy's name to get 'status'.

9. Behead a noise to get 'an old boat'.

10. Behead an insult to get 'a relative'.

11. Behead a colour to get 'a liquid'.

12. Behead a fabric to get 'a kind'.

◉ Answer on page 125.

NOW TRY THIS

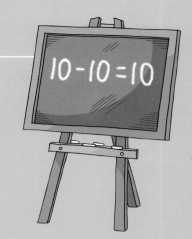

Find a way in which you can take ten from ten and have ten still remaining. If the answer does not come to you immediately, in spite of giving it some serious thought, you can try putting it to one side and letting your unconscious mind work it out. Of course, the question does involve a trick of some sort; you may well find that if you let your unconscious mull it over, the answer will suddenly appear.

◉ Answer on page 125.

 ## QUICK ON THE DRAW

Now use your imagination to turn each of the nine shapes below into a picture.

THE LAND OF NOD

Sleep is hugely important to us, although we are still not sure what its real purpose is. We do know that if we do not get enough sleep, we suffer.

At first we are simply tired, grumpy and anxious, but if the sleep deprivation continues, we will start to develop symptoms of severe mental disturbance. In extreme cases, where people are deprived of sleep over a long period, they may die.

As we have already seen, the unconscious mind is where creativity takes place. The only time we are aware of visiting this area of the mind is during our dreams. We all dream, every night. Some people are very aware of their dreams and remember them in detail; others say that they never dream, but this is not so. They simply don't recall their dreams when they wake up. The first dream of the night is the shortest, and may last no more than ten minutes or so. After eight hours of sleep, dreams can last from forty-five minutes to an hour.

Dreams occur during Rapid Eye Movement (REM) sleep. If you watch someone who is having a dream, you can actually see the eyes moving under the eyelids. During an REM period, it is common to have more than one dream. The dreams are separated by short arousals that are usually forgotten. Sleep researchers tell us that dreams are not recalled unless the sleeper awakens directly from the dream, rather than after going on to other stages of sleep.

SLEEP AND CREATIVITY

What has all this to do with creativity? Dreams may be about our fears and anxieties, but sometimes they contain the answers to problems that have been bothering us. In some instances, these will be creative problems to which we have so far failed to find an answer. If we are alert to what the unconscious tells us, we may well find the solutions we seek. Dream messages nearly always arrive in a disguised form, however, so the meaning may not be immediately apparent. This is why it is necessary to take careful note of dreams in order to work out what messages they contain.

LUCID DREAMING

There is a technique known as lucid dreaming in which (although you are asleep and dreaming) you know that you are dreaming and you are able to take charge of the dream and steer it in whatever direction you want it to go. The advantages of this are enormous. In a dream there are no limits to what you can do: you can fly, walk through walls, speak any language you wish or even visit other worlds. The opportunities for creative thinking are almost limitless for someone who possesses such abilities.

INSTRUCTIONS FOR LUCID DREAMING

- The first essential is to spend time increasing your dream awareness. At the very least, when you wake up, spend the first few minutes recalling your dreams and jotting down notes.

- The next step is to learn to look for what are called 'dream signs'. The problem with dreams is that while we are involved in them, they often seem completely normal. The fact that the sky is green and you are wearing a tuxedo and speaking Russian will not faze you one bit. These departures from normality are called dream signs and you have to train yourself to look for them.

- Next, you have to train yourself to use a sign that will tell you that you are dreaming. This can be absolutely anything you please, though it needs to be something you would not normally do. For example, you might decide that once you suspect yourself of dreaming, you could tug your left earlobe with your right hand.

- Finally, you need to learn how to prolong a lucid dream. The problem is that many people, as soon as they realize they are dreaming, tend to wake up. This is definitely not the aim. Lucid dreamers use a technique called 'dream spinning' to combat this: the moment they realize that they are dreaming, they make their dream body spin like a ballet dancer. This may sound a trifle eccentric, but experienced lucid dreamers insist that it is the best way to prolong a dream.

CREATIVE TIP

Ask a dumb question and you may look stupid for five minutes. Fail to ask it and you will be stupid for ever.

CREATIVITY FROM CONFUSION

In everyday life, the mind behaves rather like a strict and humourless teacher put in charge of a group of boisterous children. It forces us to think in a rather plodding, one-thing-at-a-time kind of way, for if the children (our thoughts) are not kept under control they will run about the place screaming, shouting and making a mess.

This might be a lot of fun, but it would interfere with everyday tasks such as driving a car or washing the dishes. For much of the time, we need to be in control of our thoughts and get them to carry out a variety of important tasks. The problem comes when we need to be creative. Creativity does not flourish in this environment. We need a way to break down the strictures that keep the rational mind under control and allow it to romp around and have a little fun. One way to do this is to make use of the power of chaos. This means using a number of methods to randomize information and give us a chance to make unusual connections that would be invisible in our normal mode of thinking.

FREE ASSOCIATION

This technique was originally used by psychoanalysts as a way of helping patients uncover their suppressed anxieties. It works well, however, as a means of liberating the conscious mind from all sorts of constraints. It is best to use a tape recorder to keep a record of each session. Start by sitting comfortably. You may want to close your eyes if that helps you to concentrate. Now, say the first word that pops into your mind. Quickly, without giving yourself any time to make rational connections, say another word, and another and another. Keep this up for as long as you wish. At first, you may find that you are a bit inhibited but, as you get used to the technique, you will find it easier to let your tongue run free and say things that you didn't intend it to say. After each session, listen to the tape several times and look out for interesting connections.

This technique has various applications. For example, if you are a writer, you could use it as a way of liberating your mind to allow characters and plot lines to develop. Alternatively, you can do this as part of a problem-solving strategy. Start with a word associated with the problem, and let your mind freewheel. You may find that you come up with words that suggest a solution. There is also a more general benefit: over time, you will begin to see patterns emerge that tell you something about the way your thought processes habitually work. This is a useful form of self-exploration that will help to deepen your understanding of your own motives and anxieties.

CREATIVE COLLAGE

This technique works well for those involved in various types of artistic creativity. Collect together a large assortment of pictures cut from magazines. You can also use all sorts of interesting odds and ends, for example a seashell, an odd-shaped stone, a brass electrical fitting or an old bottle stopper. Find a piece of board. Now comes the fun bit: arranging your materials on the board. Try lots of different arrangements until you find one that is really striking. When you are happy with your collage, stick everything in place.

Making a collage is a good way to relax and get yourself into a creative state of mind. If you examine the collage carefully, you may also find that you have unconsciously expressed thoughts and feelings that you can press into use as part of a creative project. And if you are really pleased with your effort, frame it and put it on the wall, give it to a friend or even sell it.

BRAINSTORMING

If you are trying to boost creativity in the workplace, the technique of brainstorming might prove valuable.

If you have never come across brainstorming before, it involves getting a group of people together with the purpose of thrashing out new ideas in a relaxed and informal atmosphere. The theory is that they should feel free to say whatever they want, no matter how silly or outrageous it might sound. The participants are encouraged to let their minds freewheel so that new and original ideas emerge. Ideally, people will be inspired by each other so that one person's crazy notion is seized on by someone else who sees how it might actually be made to work. This is the theory and, in recent years, brainstorming has become a very popular way of trying to generate new ideas. Sadly, not all brainstorms are as productive as they should be. In theory it looks easy to organize a successful

IN A GOOD BRAINSTORM THE PARTICIPANTS SHOULD:

- Feel relaxed.
- Exhibit genuine enthusiasm.
- Be unafraid of speaking in front of colleagues and senior managers.
- Be confident enough to propose apparently crazy ideas.
- Be willing to ask silly questions.
- Be confident that any good ideas they propose will not be stolen by others.
- Be confident that any criticisms they make will not be held against them in future.
- Be confident that they will not be ridiculed by colleagues.

brainstorming session, but in practice it is really quite difficult. To see why, you need to appreciate the characteristics of a good session.

In a corporate setting, these conditions can be hard to achieve. People who are used to a corporate atmosphere are often quite suspicious of each other and there are always undercurrents of rivalry and jealousy that make a free exchange of ideas difficult. In many companies, there is a formal, businesslike atmosphere that discourages people from behaviour that might look silly or frivolous. Even in more laid-back companies, it would take quite a lot of courage for an employee to say something radical in front of

HERE ARE SOME TIPS FOR ORGANIZING A PRODUCTIVE SESSION:

1. **Groups should be kept small.**
   If you have more than a dozen participants, the atmosphere will not be intimate enough.

2. **Seating is important.**
   Seat people around a table so that they can interact easily. If you use a more formal seating arrangement, people will feel inhibited.

3. **Make the aims clear.**
   You must make sure that people understand the purpose of the session. At the start, outline what you hope to achieve.

4. **Don't evaluate.**
   At this stage, all ideas are good. If someone says something wacky, that's fine. Just note everything and keep it for later.

5. **Make sure that participants listen to each other.**
   Show all participants respect and make sure that others follow your lead. Encourage people to enlarge on the ideas offered by other participants. Be very clear that no one is to ridicule suggestions made by other participants.

6. **Use the china egg technique.**
   Farmers sometimes use a china egg to encourage hens to lay. You must do a similar thing. Lead the way by offering some wild, unconventional ideas. If people see you do it, they will feel free to follow your example.

7. **Try to generate as many ideas as possible.**
   At this stage, quantity is important. The quality of the ideas can be assessed later.

8. **Keep the atmosphere informal and relaxed.**
   Meet somewhere away from the usual working environment, preferably not a conference centre (because they all look like extensions of the office). Consider providing a meal – eating will relax the participants and they'll feel the need to repay your generosity by coming up with ideas.

9. **Keep them interested.**
   While making sure that participants don't stray from the task in hand, try to keep them relaxed and interested. Have breaks during which people can chat informally.

10. **Keep a record.**
    Record the session, preferably using a tape recorder, rather than having someone take notes. Having your words written down is a bit intimidating, but people soon forget about a tape recorder.

senior colleagues. For such a session to work, it needs to be headed by a senior figure who takes the lead in creating the right atmosphere.

At its best, brainstorming is a wonderful demonstration of how chaos can be used to encourage creative thought. If you get the right group of people there will be a lively, thought-provoking discussion in which all will feel free to participate. The outcome will be a mass of ideas that can then be sorted and evaluated using the idea shuffling technique (see page 76). A bad brainstorming session, however, is not just useless but actually damaging. I have been present at sessions where people competed madly to get the boss's attention and approval, poured scorn on colleagues' ideas and behaved as though they were deadly rivals (which they were) rather than a team fired by enthusiasm and cooperation. So be warned: if you brainstorm you must take great pains to get it right or you may end up doing more harm than good.

RANDOMIZING

Many creative people suffer the frustration of not being able to break out of their normal mode of thought to embrace the creative notions that seem to hover all around them.

In the early twentieth century, some writers experimented with breaking down the formal structure of their text. The theory was that once text was liberated, new connections would be perceived. The technique involved taking pages of text, cutting them up and then reassembling them in a random order. Naturally, our commonsense mind will dismiss the randomized text as mere nonsense deprived of all meaning. Enthusiasts for the technique argued that it created a new and more vibrant text that was full of previously undiscovered meanings. Why not try it? The technique need not be confined to works of fiction. You can take any sort of text and randomize it in this way to see whether it throws up new meanings.

IDEA SHUFFLING

This is a rather less radical technique and one that I have used many times. It works best if you use a program such as Microsoft PowerPoint, but you can also use a word-processing program or even, if you are not comfortable with computers, pieces of blank card. Start by jotting down ideas at random. Do not make any attempt to evaluate your ideas at this stage. If using PowerPoint, create a new slide for each idea. This part of the process may take anything from a few minutes to many weeks. When you feel that you have enough ideas to work with, you can start to shuffle them about.

PowerPoint allows you to show all your slides at once and then move them around. If you are word processing, you can cut and paste text to create a similar effect. Soon, you will start to see themes emerge. Now you can start to evaluate your ideas, promoting the strong ones to a more prominent position and relegating others to the bottom of the heap. This is the most important part of the process, because this is where you decide the shape of the finished product. Don't hurry to reach a conclusion and rearrange your ideas as much as you like. Have the confidence to make bold creative decisions. If you decide to try something really radical, always save a copy of the current layout before making huge alterations. That way, if you later decide that your bright idea was a failure, you can always revert to the earlier version without having lost anything.

Eventually, you will end up with an outline that satisfies you. No matter how much you like the outline you've created, never regard it as set in stone. The essence of creativity is to allow ideas to develop and change freely throughout the process. So as you start putting your project together, consider the outline as fluid and still open to change.

USING CHAOS TO CREATE A PLOT

When I teach creative writing, there is one exercise that always proves popular. It involves making up a story that uses a set of words. Try it yourself. Your plotline must also include the following:

- A missed opportunity.
- Mistaken identity.
- Something hidden.

- A shocking turn of events.
- Sibling rivalry.

There are no right answers to this exercise; just make sure that you use all the words and plot elements you've been given. When you've done it once, see whether you can do it again using a different plot. You might also find that it's fun to try the exercise in a group.

PORTRAIT	TRUCK	SINGING
BLEARY	CONFIDENCE	CERTAINTY
ROMANTIC	HAPPY	POLICE
VALUABLE	FLOWERS	UNAWARE
PHILOSOPHER	BELL	DIAMOND
FRANTIC	AMMUNITION	CHOCOLATE
WELCOME	REPAIR	CALCULATOR
BORDER	BALANCE	GRANDMOTHER
CONFIDENCE	FORTUNE	FADED
RABBIT	SANDWICH	
CARPENTER	CREATION	

PLOTTING A NOVEL – ORDER FROM CHAOS

Chaos is a useful tool in creativity, but it is important not to make it an end in itself. Sometimes people get so caught up in the fun of creating chaos that they lose sight of the fact that it needs to be brought under control if it is to produce anything useful. Once you reach the stage where you have a good store of ideas, you need to start bringing some sort of order to the chaos.

Here is another technique that I use when teaching plot construction. If writing is not the sort of creativity that interests you, it doesn't matter – this technique can be adapted to a variety of uses.

- First, state the whole of your idea in no more than 100 words. You might find this quite difficult, because it calls for a high degree of compression. That, however, is the point – it will force you to extract, from a mass of thoughts, the ones that form the bare bones of the project. Imagine that you will use this 100-word summary to sell the idea to someone. You need to state the whole idea as clearly and attractively as possible.

- Now you are ready to produce a more elaborate version of your summary. Even so, do not write more than a few hundred words. The mistake many people make when they start creative work is to produce a mass of material that is intended to show just how much work they have done. They hope that when they try to get a buyer for their idea, the sheer volume of material will act as an inducement. Nothing could be further from the truth. The sort of people who buy creative ideas have a very limited attention span and will expect you to convince them in as few words as possible.

- You do, however, have to be able to demonstrate that your work is complete – at least in outline form. It must have a beginning that is intriguing enough to persuade the reader to keep on reading. It must have dramatic tension (i.e. things have to go wrong and then the characters must try to put them right) and there must be an ending. This may seem obvious, but you would be amazed at how many novels arrive on an editor's desk lacking one or more of these vital ingredients.

> **CREATIVE TIP**
> First the chaos; then the production of order from chaos. In this way, interesting ideas may be born.

- Now you are ready to start adding flesh to the bones of your project. Let's assume that your project is a novel. At this stage, you should have a list of all the main characters, and you need to write a biography for each of them. You may well not use all the information in the biographies, but it is important to know everything about the characters so that you understand what influences their behaviour in the story.

- You are now ready to write a chapter-by-chapter breakdown of the whole book. It is very important to do this. If you start writing without any clear idea of where you are going, you'll find that the plot meanders. Do not, however, regard your chapter breakdown as sacred. It is very important to be prepared to make alterations as the plot develops. You will no doubt go through numerous versions of the plot before you hit on the final one.

- One complication that most fiction authors experience is that the characters are not, as you might think, mere models that you can push around as you please. Once you have created them, they become people with personalities of their own, and they will insist on doing things their own way. People who have not worked with fiction before often find this idea foolish. However, once you have tried dealing with fictional characters, you will soon discover that I'm telling the truth!

EXPLORING THE DEPTHS

In most activities, we are largely in control of what we do. Our conscious intentions are closely reflected in the results we obtain. So if you want to build a wall, fix your car, take the kids for a day by the sea or buy your partner a present, you have no difficulty in making a plan and carrying it out.

The conscious mind is quite capable of governing such activities. Creativity, however, is utterly different, for it depends very largely on the activities of the unconscious mind. This makes it strange, mysterious, magical and profoundly irritating. It is galling to find that one of our most important faculties, on which our whole civilization depends, is largely beyond our control.

Let's think of the mind as an ocean. We can see the surface perfectly well and at certain times, such as when we are asleep, we can penetrate a short way into deeper waters. Most of the ocean is simply too deep and dark for us to visit – but the murky depths are no mere void. All the evidence suggests that, on the contrary, the unconscious is an area of unceasing activity. It works day and night whether we are active, relaxing or soundly asleep. All sorts of things swim around in the deep and sometimes some of them emerge into conscious thought. These can be thoughts, dreams, memories, ideas, anxieties – literally anything and everything you can think of. The odd thing is the apparently random way in which thoughts emerge from the subconscious.

Some of what happens is fairly straightforward – for example, if you have just seen an old friend it is not surprising if, for some time afterwards, memories of time you spent together keep popping up to the surface. You might even start to have associated memories that are not directly connected to that person. For example, if the friend was someone you knew at school, it would not be unusual to conjure up memories of teachers who had a strong influence on you. The mind, however, does not always act in such a logical way. Very often, thoughts pop up quite unbidden, and for reasons we cannot fathom. It is a little unsettling to realize that the mind is concerning itself with a whole host of things that you know nothing about. If you want to engage in any sort of creative activity you need to learn the tricks of fishing for ideas in this dark, mysterious ocean.

We have already looked at techniques that allow us to access the twilight zone that exists on the border between the conscious mind and the unconscious, but now we need to take a look at ways to get to the deeper levels where creativity resides.

CREATIVE VISUALIZATION

Much nonsense is talked about visualization, but used sensibly, it does have an important role to play. Some people are natural visualizers; others do not find it easy to think in pictures. Natural visualizers, for example, will automatically conjure up vivid and detailed pictures of settings and characters when they read a book. Or when a friend describes her holiday, a natural visualizer will automatically create a vision of that place in their mind's eye. With practice, visualization can become an effortless process for everyone.

Visualizing is valuable because it allows us to experience vicariously situations that we are unable, for a variety of reasons, to experience at first hand. Those who perfect the technique often find that they can 'see' a solution to a problem even when they have been unable to discover it by the normal processes of reasoning.

SEVEN STEPS TO VISUALIZATION

The following steps show how to use visualization to assist in a creative project.

1. Choose a room where you can be quiet and feel comfortable.

2. Sit in a comfortable position, or lie down if you prefer. Relax. Have background music on if you find that it helps.

3. Close your eyes, and let your mind start to build a picture of the project you are working on.

4. The aim is to build the most detailed picture possible of your project. Try to see what it will look like when it is finished.

5. Don't spend time sorting out worries and problems. Those things can be dealt with elsewhere. This is the place for creating a positive vision that will encourage you in your efforts.

6. Make full use of your powers of imagination. For example, if you need expensive equipment, then as long as you can imagine it, you can have it.

7. Visualization is not magic. Some people are keen to believe that if you visualize a completed project it will in some magic way become reality. It won't. Visualization encourages you by providing a positive vision of what you can achieve, but it is never a substitute for action.

CONCENTRATION

Many people think that creative work is all about chilling out and having wonderful ideas while in a state of mental calm. This is certainly one face of creativity, but it is not the only one.

Once you have the ideas, it takes hard work to translate them into reality, and hard work takes concentration. For some strange reason, it is popularly assumed that concentration is possible merely by an act of will. Few of us are ever taught to concentrate. Parents of youngsters who show signs of being easily distracted are often told by teachers, 'He must learn to concentrate', but no advice is ever forthcoming about how to do this. Here are some ways in which you can strengthen your powers of concentration:

⦿ Manage your time carefully. When you start a job, estimate how long it is going to take you. If it is a large job, you may want to split it up into several phases, with a time estimate for each of these.

⦿ Once you have done the estimate, try very hard to stick to it. In the beginning, you may find that your estimates are wide of the mark, but you will become more accurate with experience.

⦿ Allow yourself breaks for a cup of coffee, but take them at a time you have decided beforehand. Don't use a break as an excuse to distract you from the work. It is

very easy, when work is not flowing smoothly, to get up and put the kettle on or phone a friend for a chat. Problems are not solved that way – all you do is postpone them and lose valuable time.

⦿ At first, you may find it difficult to work in this way. Many of us have become used to punctuating the day with multiple distractions designed to take the tedium out of work. However, if you persist, you will find yourself richly rewarded. You will start to achieve more and your work will be of a higher quality than before.

⦿ In a working environment, it is often difficult to stop people from distracting each other. If you are in a senior position in your company, you might consider things you could do to help. The main one would be to cut drastically the number of meetings you hold. The office meeting is a monster worthy of Frankenstein. It devours huge amounts of time and frequently achieves nothing.

⦿ Two other major distractions are e-mail and Microsoft PowerPoint. These are both excellent tools, without which our workplaces would be much poorer. Sadly, they are also wonderful ways to waste time. Any sensible boss would clamp down on the amount of time people spend sending each other e-mails or compiling PowerPoint presentations.

ROUND 1

Look at the list of letters below and try to find pairs that have one letter between them in the alphabet (e.g. A C, E G and K M would be three such pairs). How many pairs are there?

```
D  E  G  I  A  M  N  P  S  T  V
X  B  E  H  T  K  M  O  Q  V  D
O  F  H  J  L  X  A  B
```

 Answer on page 125.

 ## ROUND 2

In this list of digits, you must pick out the pairs that add up to 10.

```
1  6  4  7  8  2  4  5  5  2  4
6  4  7  9  1  2  8  3  4  5  2
6  4  3  7  8  9  1  2  8  3  2
4  6  4
```

 Answer on page 125.

 ## ROUND 3

Now try to find pairs of letters separated by two places in the alphabet (e.g. A D, H K, P S).

```
S  D  G  K  L  O  R  U  V  X  J
M  P  D  C  T  W  J  P  Y  F  I
L  O  A  T  S  W  Z  B  D
```

Answer on page 125.

ROUND 4

Here, you must find sets of three digits that add up to 12.

```
1  5  2  5  3  8  4  6  2  9  0
3  7  8  5  3  7  2  4  6  6  2  1
2  4  5  3  2  8  2  4  6  2  3
3  4
```

Answer on page 125.

ROUND 5

Finally, take a look at this unusual maze. Why unusual? Because most mazes have only one correct solution, but this one has hundreds. Can you work out how many? This is a task involving real concentration. But beware! Since this maze was first invented, it has been blamed for sending people mad.

Answer: See page 125.

MEDITATION

It is unfortunate that in Western society, meditation is known only for its connection with Eastern mystical religious practice.

The popular view of meditation is polarized between those who believe it is an almost magical technique for attaining enlightenment, and those who think it is a load of nonsense. Neither view is especially helpful. In fact, meditation is not a single phenomenon, but a large number of techniques, that are used for a wide variety of purposes. There is nothing remotely magical about any of them. They all make use of the mind's enormous power to help us in various ways.

A SIMPLE MEDITATION

Here are instructions for a simple meditation technique that anybody can use. It is completely safe and easy to do, and has great benefits.

- You need a room where you can be quiet and won't get distracted.

- Choose a time when you are unlikely to have callers and, if possible, turn off your phone.

- The room you choose should be light, airy and neither too warm nor too cool.

- Sit comfortably on an upright chair, with a cushion if necessary. Don't lean against the back of the chair. Sit up straight, but not so straight that you feel strained.

- Tuck in your chin slightly, close your eyes and fold your hands in your lap.

- Now start to focus on your breathing. Breathe normally through your nose. Keep your mouth lightly shut.

- Try to keep your mind on your breathing by counting your breaths. Count on each out-breath. When you get to five, go back to the beginning again.

- To begin with, you will be surprised how hard it is to do this without being distracted. You'll find yourself constantly bothered by itches, noises coming from outdoors and wandering thoughts. Every time you feel distracted, just gently guide your thoughts back to your breathing.

- Eventually, you will find that you enter a state of deep relaxation.

DON'T GO TO SLEEP!

- It is entirely natural to sleep when you feel relaxed, and therefore you have to learn to stay awake. If you keep your upright posture, this will help you to stay alert. (If you do fall asleep, try to carry on with your meditation when you wake up. You may find that a brief nap refreshes you.) If you really can't get over your sleepiness, give up and try another time when you are more rested.

- Once you have mastered the art of entering a meditative state without sleeping, you can make it part of your creative process and use it to assist in creative projects that you are undertaking.

- While meditating, begin to examine the creative project in question. It is important that you don't start to analyse it or worry about problems you are having. That is not what meditation is all about. Try to keep the project in your mind and simply examine it as though you were a stranger seeing it for the first time. Don't evaluate or criticize, just LOOK.

- While in a state of deep meditation, you are in close proximity to the unconscious mind but, because you are fully conscious, when you bring your meditation to an end you will remember any thoughts that occurred to you.

- This is the point at which you will start to have useful insights into your project. Aspects of your work that have so far eluded you will suddenly become apparent. You may well find that answers to problems that have been bothering you will now pop into your mind.

- Meditate regularly. As a beginner, it is only necessary to do ten minutes (which will seem like an eternity). As you progress, the meditation can be extended to twenty or thirty minutes.

- The benefits of meditation are manifold. You will find that you feel more relaxed, more able to think creatively and that your general health will improve.

Now try the concentration game on page 83. It requires no special skill other than the ability to force yourself to concentrate for a prolonged period. There are five rounds to the game, which you must complete in the given time. For each round, the rules are slightly different.

BIORHYTHMS AND CREATIVITY

Some years ago, there was a craze for the 'science' of biorhythms. The idea had been around for a long time but was suddenly seized upon as the latest New Age craze.

The theory is that our lives operate on three cycles – the physical, the emotional and the intellectual. These cycles start at birth and continue throughout our lives. The idea is that at any given time we may, for example, be in an intellectual phase whilst our physical powers are at a low ebb and our emotional cycle is just starting an upswing. Practitioners of this pseudo-science believe that it is possible to discover each individual's biorhythm cycle and therefore predict how he or she is feeling on any given day. What is more, fans of biorhythms believe that we can

obtain interesting information about our relationships with other people by comparing biorhythm cycles. One particularly hilarious book on the subject focused on a couple of celebrity marriages and discussed at length the way in which the couples involved were ideally suited to each other. The effect was spoiled a little by the author's choice of couples – Woody Allen and Mia Farrow, and Princess Diana and Prince Charles.

But wait! Not everything about biorhythms is nonsense. The truth is that we do experience regular changes in our physical, emotional and intellectual lives. How many people feel low-spirited and unenthusiastic first thing on a Monday morning? Probably the vast majority. How many feel light-hearted and enthusiastic just before going home for the weekend on a Friday? Again, most

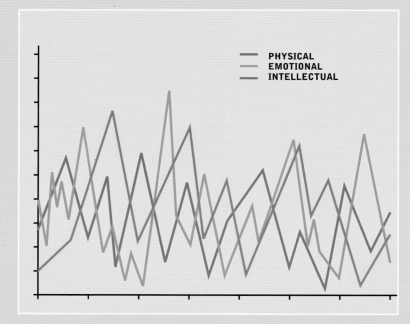

PHYSICAL
EMOTIONAL
INTELLECTUAL

This shows how biorhythms are supposed to work with our mental, physical and emotional abilities rising and falling in a regular pattern. Nothing could be further from the truth.

	0700	0900	1100	1200	1300	1400	1500	1700	1900	2200
MON Physical										
Emotional										
Intellectual										
TUES Physical										
Emotional										
Intellectual										
WED Physical										
Emotional										
Intellectual										
THUR Physical										
Emotional										
Intellectual										
FRI Physical										
Emotional										
Intellectual										
SAT Physical										
Emotional										
Intellectual										
SUN Physical										
Emotional										
Intellectual										

Our mental, physical and emotional abilities do alter over time but the process is not as orderly as biorhythm enthusiasts would have us believe. It is possible, however, to find times when we regularly feel a marked rise or fall of one of these aspects of our being. Knowing about these peaks and troughs is useful when planning future activities.

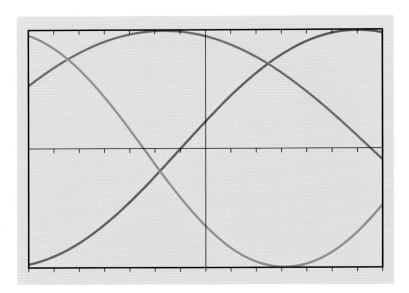

people would admit to feeling like this. But we also have our own individual good and bad times. Some people leap out of bed eager to greet a new day, while others struggle to get their brains in gear. Some people function beautifully all day, as long as they are able to take a short nap after lunch.

In order to understand the nature of these changes in biorhythms, we have to plot them accurately. This seems an eminently sensible idea and well worth the tiny amount of trouble that it takes. Simply photocopy the chart on the previous page four times and fill it in each day for four weeks. To complete it, contemplate your physical, emotional and intellectual state throughout the day and award yourself marks out of ten according to the intensity of each state.

The theory of biorhythms is that they rise and fall in a regular pattern like sine waves (see the biorhythm chart on page 86). As anyone with any sense knows, this just isn't so. Our moods can change rapidly for a variety of reasons. If you take the trouble to

chart your moods, you will find that you have regular peaks and troughs throughout the week. You may discover that Monday afternoon is a time when your intellect is powerful, but emotional and physical states are a bit low. This perhaps indicates that it is a good time to sit quietly, thinking about things, rather than trying to communicate with others. On the other hand, you may find that on Thursdays you often feel physically active but don't seem too keen on intellectual pursuits. It would be interesting to plot your findings on a simple graph. It might end up looking something like the chart shown above.

The data you gain from this exercise should allow you to identify times in each week when your intellectual, emotional and physical powers are at their peak. You will probably discover that there are particular times when you regularly feel inspired to perform creative tasks, and other times when it would be better to expend your energies in some other way.

LIBIDO AND MORTIDO

Sex and creativity have had a long and steamy affair. (Renoir famously remarked, 'I paint with my prick'!) The relationship between the two appears blatantly in many paintings, sculptures, novels, films and plays with a sexual theme.

But it appears much more subtly in the way in which creative people are affected by their work. The act of creation seems closely linked, at some unconscious level, with the act of procreation. To put it at its crudest, creative people get a sexual buzz from their work. This is one reason they are, quite literally, passionate about what they are doing. Their deep commitment to their work echoes the commitment one feels for a lover. Furthermore, in the post-Freudian age, we know that both consciously and unconsciously people may express their deepest feelings through their creative work. This creative urge is normally called 'libido'. Libido also describes sexual desire.

DESTRUCTIVE URGES

It is often overlooked, however, that according to Freud, libido has a partner. This is the destructive death instinct called 'mortido'. Psychologically, there has always been controversy over whether mortido actually exists. Do we really have a mental component that urges us towards death? In some cultures, this idea is accepted without question. In India, for example, the dance of

Shiva expresses both the creative and destructive urges simultaneously.

Why should destruction be important creatively? Because it gives us the urge to tear up that which is old and out of date, and to make something new in its place. It also gives us the courage to junk work that is not up to standard and strive to make something better.

There is a well-known Japanese story about a potter who finished a piece of work, placed it in the middle of her studio, burned incense and contemplated it. Day after day, she examined the new work from every angle. Then, after some weeks, she came to a decision. She fetched a hammer and smashed the new work to pieces. To do such a thing required a huge amount of courage and dedication. It would have been easier for her to accept the piece (and probably no one would have said anything because she was a very famous artist). But in the end, she could not accept work that was not up to her very high standards.

Learning to smash things that need smashing is a part of creativity that is often overlooked. It is very easy to accept what we have made, but it is far more difficult to have the courage to destroy things. It is also easy to accept the work of others and not make waves by criticizing it. But mortido urges us to smash up what is second rate and to do away with anything that has served its turn, and if we are to be truly creative, this is a lesson we must learn.

THE DOORS OF PERCEPTION

Books on creativity tend to avoid the role drugs and alcohol have played in the lives of many creative people. This is entirely understandable as no one wants to appear to be condoning or encouraging behaviour that is unwise or even illegal. But to dodge the issue would be just plain dishonest.

A list of all the creative people who have become notorious for their reliance on booze and illegal substances would make a very long chapter all on its own. Another list of lives ruined or brought to an untimely end would be almost as long. This is by no means a recent phenomenon. The Chinese poet Li Po, who lived during the T'ang dynasty (618 – 906), was famous for his love affair with the bottle and eventually drowned while drunkenly trying to embrace a reflection of the moon in the waters of the Yangtse river. There has been no shortage of creative types eager to follow his example.

What is the special attraction that drugs hold for creative people? First, there is the task of breaking down the barrier between the normal everyday mind and the creative force that lies hidden in the unconscious. This is and always has been an enormous problem. People have tried all sorts of methods to liberate the mind and allow the creative force to flow. Without question drugs do help to get rid of inhibitions and, in many cases, they allow users to see things that would normally lie hidden. They also conjure up fantasies of such power and beauty that they can seem like divine revelations. For people who spend much of their lives struggling to force the unconscious to yield its secrets, the prospect of a quick means of achieving this aim is very seductive.

Second, creative work often involves examining life far more closely than most of us would dare to do. Our life is a great mystery and it is the mission of creative people to explore that mystery in as many ways as possible. Sometimes, however, that exploration leads people along dark and dangerous paths. Life can seem unbearably bleak and those who examine this aspect too closely often come to harm. In these circumstances drugs may offer a temporary respite from an overdose of reality. In reality, of course, the drugs themselves only exacerbate the problem.

At one time the use of drugs to enhance creativity involved only occasional use by a few isolated individuals. If we look back to the nineteenth century, for example, we find people such as Samuel Taylor Coleridge who famously saw a vision while under the influence of opium that he tried to capture in his poem *Kubla Khan*. As long as drug use was the vice of a few eccentrics it was a very minor danger. In the early 1950s, however, the British writer Aldous Huxley experimented with mescalin, a drug capable of producing psychedelic experiences. What happened to him is described in his essay entitled *The Doors of Perception* (the title came from the poet William Blake who said, 'If the doors of perception were cleansed every thing would appear to man as it is, infinite. For man has closed himself up, till he sees all things thru' narrow chinks of his cavern'). Huxley's work had a huge influence on the '60s generation; in fact the band The Doors chose their name as a direct reference to his essay.

Suddenly there was a drug explosion. The taking of drugs was seen not just as a recreational activity but as an easily accessible route to higher levels of consciousness. No matter how much politicians, police and parents disapproved, the younger generation felt they had found something wonderful that could transform their lives for the better. They were encouraged in this belief by older people like Dr Timothy Leary who memorably told them to, 'Turn on, tune in and drop out.'

The fact that drugs were extremely dangerous made no difference to their

popularity. Famous names of that generation such as Jimi Hendrix and Janis Joplin may have died as a result of their drug use but that did nothing to persuade the younger generation to give them up and that attitude has not only persisted but flourished. Now the Western world has a huge drug problem that simply cannot be solved. Although there is a constant call for tougher and tougher sentences on drug dealers and users, there is in fact nothing that will deter a huge number of people from abusing substances.

Here we are not concerned with the moral or legal aspects of drug taking but only with its effect on creativity. The central question we need to ask is, 'Does taking drugs make you more creative?' There are countless musicians, painters, poets and writers who would say it does. The evidence, however, is not compelling. Looking back at the '60s it is hard to see anything worthwhile that was added to creative thought by drug use. The pretty psychedelic patterns have faded now and much of the music has been forgotten.

Drugs and alcohol make people feel that they are being creative but, sadly, any insights are fleeting and do not translate readily into any form that can be expressed by art. On the other hand the effects of drug use on health are all too easily seen. Not only do young people still die as a result of drug use, but some of those who survived the '60s are visibly damaged by their past excesses. So, if you want to be creative, don't do drugs.

A BRIGHT IDEA IS ONLY THE BEGINNING

Stories about how inventive individuals come up with bright ideas that sweep the world are all too common. They all tend to follow a certain plot in which the zany, creative inventor suddenly comes upon a wild idea (often by accident) and immediately recognizes its world-beating potential.

From there, it is but a short step to fame and fortune. Such stories are popular because they create the illusion that all you need to be a successful creative individual is a sudden flash of inspiration. This is very far from the truth and completely ignores all the long, hard slog in getting from the initial bright idea to the finished product.

THE BIRO

Let's look, for example, at the story of the ballpoint pen. Most people know that a Hungarian journalist called Laszlo Biro invented the ballpoint and gave his name to it. Some people have also heard the story that Biro got his bright idea for the pen from watching printing presses at work. He reasoned that it should be possible to make a pen in which a tiny ball-bearing could press ink on to paper in a similar manner to the way in which printing presses work. In fact, the true story is quite different.

The search for a new type of pen had been going on for some years. The trouble with fountain pens was that the ink flow was often uneven, and the ink would sometimes dry and clog the pen, which would then need to be stripped down and thoroughly cleaned before it would work again. There was another problem with the fountain pen that, although it might seem unimportant, was to have far-reaching effects: it had a tendency to flood when it was used on aeroplanes. The significance of this will be seen later.

In fact, the idea of the ballpoint pen was not at all new. In 1888 an American leather tanner called John Loud patented a marker pen with an ink reservoir and a roller ball that he used to apply ink to leather hides. Loud's pen never went into production, and over the next thirty years there were well over 300 patents for ball-type pens that were no more successful than his. This demonstrates an important aspect of creative thought – the fact that frequently there are several (or sometimes many) people who are all struggling with the same problem at the same time.

There were a couple of problems with the ballpoint that no one had been able to solve. It had so far been impossible to produce an ink that was neither too thick nor too liquid, and that would spread evenly when rolled on paper. Also, no one had come up with a ball that would run smoothly without sticking.

Laszlo Biro had a couple of ideas that he hoped would solve these problems. He knew from his newspaper work that newspaper ink is quick-drying and leaves the paper dry and smudge-free almost instantly. His second idea was to use a tiny ball-bearing to spread the ink. This would not only act as a cap to prevent the ink from drying in the pen, but it would also control the rate at which the ink was released.

Laszlo worked with his brother Georg, a chemist, and in 1943 they took out a patent with the European Patent Office and made the first successful ballpoint pens. They managed to make an ink of the right consistency and to find (in Sweden) a supplier of ball-bearings that were tough and smooth enough for the job they had to do.

It was at this stage that a new advantage of the ballpoint was discovered – unlike the fountain pen, it did not flood when used in aircraft. The British government immediately bought the rights to the pen, so that biros could be used by the Royal Air Force. The Second World War proved to be a wonderful opportunity for the Biro company to show just what their pens could do. This demonstrates another important facet of creative thought – for a good idea to become successful, it must arrive at the right time. The war gave the ballpoint pen the chance to prove its superiority, in toughness and durability, to traditional designs.

After the war, the idea for the ballpoint spread rapidly.

BIC

Once the principle of the ballpoint was well established, the next step was for someone to make an inexpensive version that would be available to everyone. In 1945, Frenchman Marcel Bich developed an industrial process for making ballpoint pens that lowered the unit cost dramatically. In 1949, Bich introduced his pens in Europe. He used the name 'BIC', which was a shortened, easy-to-remember version of his name.

A decade later, BIC pens were first sold in America and, to begin with, they were not popular. The problem was that there were too many cheap and unreliable ballpoints being made. In order to convince the Americans that BIC pens were different, a national TV campaign was launched using the slogan 'Writes First Time, Every Time!' The BIC pen was first priced at 29 cents, but very quickly came down to 10 cents, and it was soon being sold in millions.

Even now, the development of the ballpoint has not ended. It was found that the cap could be swallowed by young children, causing them to choke. As a result there has been an ongoing quest for a cap design that would allow a child to breathe even if the cap were to become accidentally lodged in the throat.

A NASTY CASE OF SCURVY

On the previous pages, we saw how the commercial success of the ballpoint pen was helped by the way in which it played a useful role in the Second World War. Not all good ideas have been fortunate enough to get a helping hand like that.

Let's look at a very different case, in which a bright idea existed and was widely publicized for many years without being taken up.

Scurvy is a very unpleasant and potentially fatal disease that afflicts those whose diet is deficient in vitamin C. It used to affect sailors in particular – they were far more likely to die from scurvy than from enemy action, storms or drowning. This painful and debilitating disease would make its victims weak, and cause them to suffer from pains in the joints. Internal haemorrhaging would produce black and blue marks on the skin. Raised red spots would appear around the hair follicles of the legs, buttocks, arms and back. The gums would haemorrhage and the tissue become weak

and spongy. The dentine (which lies beneath tooth enamel) would rot, causing the teeth to loosen, and thus making eating painful.

To give some idea of the scale of the problem caused by scurvy, a British report published in 1600 estimated that in the previous twenty years, some 10,000 sailors had been destroyed by the disease. There were various theories about what caused scurvy, and many of them were very wide of the mark. For example, because the disease caused depression and lethargy, it was assumed that it was the result of 'laziness' among sailors and could therefore be cured by making the poor devils work harder.

However, there were serious attempts to find a cure. In 1535 Jacques Cartier came across a herbal remedy (using brewed spruce tips and bark) that he claimed was an effective treatment. In 1652 John Josselyn wrote of a Native American cure for the disease. The fact that these claims were never seriously pursued is not entirely

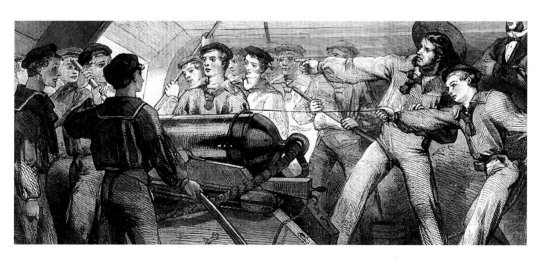

surprising. There was never any shortage of quack remedies and no real reason why medical authorities should have paid much attention to the claims of herbalists.

FINDING A CURE

However, by the eighteenth century, there was some real progress in the study of scurvy. In 1747 James Lind, a British naval doctor on board HMS Salisbury, sailing from England to the Plymouth Colony, decided to carry out an experiment that would test various remedies. He had twelve infected sailors on board, and he divided them into six groups of two. The six groups shared the same diet but each was given a different dietary supplement. These were as follows:

⦿ A daily quart of apple juice.

⦿ Twenty-five drops of elixir vitriol (an alarming concoction containing sulphuric acid and aromatic herbs).

⦿ Two spoonfuls of vinegar, three times a day.

⦿ A mixture of herbs and spices.

⦿ Half a pint of seawater daily.

⦿ Two oranges and one lemon daily.

The two men who were given citrus fruit improved rapidly and within six days they were fit to resume their duties. The men given apple juice showed a slight improvement, but none of the others improved at all. Lind concluded that there was an ingredient in citrus fruit that was an effective cure for scurvy.

It is well known that British sailors were given a daily ration of lime or lemon juice (which was the origin of the nickname 'limeys') and that this preventative medicine eliminated scurvy throughout the Navy. However, this measure was not taken until 1795 – nearly half a century after Lind carried out his experiment!

PUTTING AN IDEA INTO PRACTICE

We often assume that the moment a bright idea appears, it is seized upon with enthusiasm and put into effect straight away. Here is a sorry tale that proves this is far from true. Lind's experiment must have been well known to naval authorities and, as he was a ship's physician, there is no reason why his claims should not have been believed. Considering the seriousness of the scurvy problem, we would expect such a significant finding to be eagerly received. Here was a simple and relatively inexpensive method of protecting the health of sailors and maintaining the efficiency of the Royal Navy. Why on earth did it take so long for such an important discovery to be put to good use?

Take this story as a warning. Just because you have a good idea that works, do not assume that you will find it easy to get your idea put into practice.

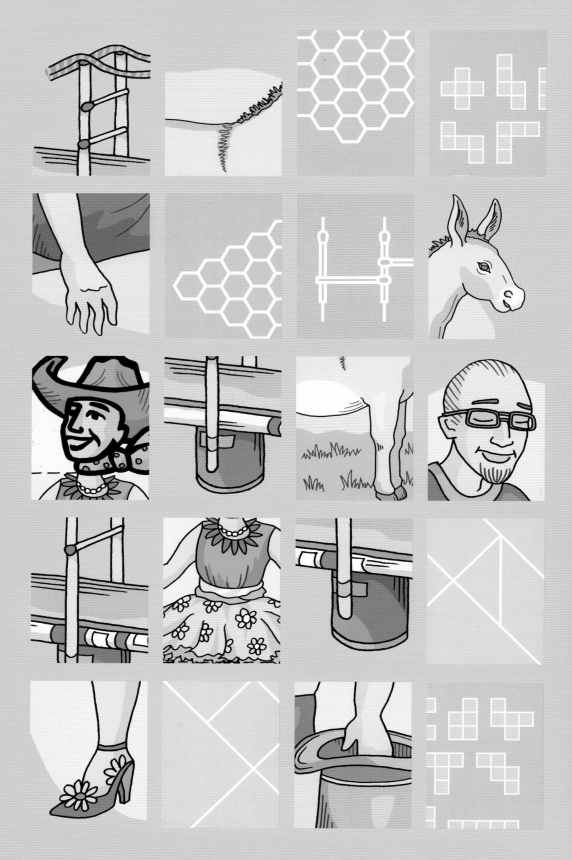

PART THREE:
CREATIVITY GAMES

In every game you'll discover that you are rewarded for unconventional thinking that takes you beyond the obvious. If you make a point of playing the games over and over you will find that the more you make demands on your creative ability the more it will produce.

The purpose of the games that follow is to encourage you to think in new ways and put you in touch with that part of the mind that produces bright ideas. Getting the right answer is not as important as thinking in unfamiliar ways. The very best thing that could happen would be if you got a completely different answer that was also correct. Once your mind has been stimulated and is in problem-solving mode it is quite likely that it will throw up the answer to some completely different problem which has nothing to do with the one you intended to work on. Why? Who knows? But you have to be on the lookout for 'bonus' thoughts and make a note of them before you forget.

'Much may be done in those little shreds and patches of time which every day produces, and which most men throw away.'

CHARLES CALEB COLTON

BRIDGE

This has nothing to do with the card game of the same name. The object of this game is quite simple – you just have to build a bridge. You can play the game in a great variety of ways, but as a general rule the simpler you make it, the more creative will be the results.

- Choose an umpire to make sure that no cheating takes place. Divide the players into teams (individual players are permitted, but that is usually less fun).

- Each team is given exactly the same materials. Use only the simplest things – old newspapers, cardboard, string, maybe a few empty cans and some sticky tape.

- Decide how long the teams will have to build their bridges.

- Decide on minimum and maximum dimensions for the bridges.

- Once the bridges have been built, there is the fun of testing them. Each bridge is tested to destruction by placing weights on it until it collapses. Keep a careful record of the weight that each bridge is able to bear.

- You will be surprised just how tough these bridges can be. Players with a little basic physics (or merely some native cunning) at their disposal will be able to build structures that perform surprisingly well.

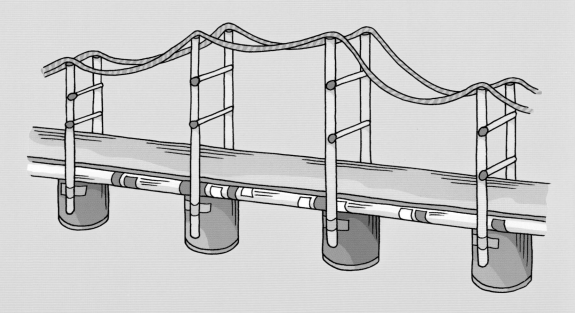

HOPSCOTCH

This is a game for two to six players and it has no connection with the playground game of the same name. You can devise versions that are suitable for both children and adults.

Each player in turn is given five themes by the other players to link together. For example, a player could be told to get from 'Sport' to 'Music' via 'Literature', 'Science' and 'Taxidermy'. The player then makes up to nine statements, and must touch on each of the themes in the order given. The other players work together to act as umpires and decide whether all the themes have been touched on, that the associations are valid and that none of the puns, jokes or allusions are too far-fetched. Marks out of 100 are given for wit and creativity.

The round described above might be played like this:

1. Football is a sport (Sport).
2. People sing at football matches (Music).
3. Songs are written.
4. Writers produce books (Literature).
5. Science is found in books (Science).
6. Biology is a science.
7. Biology studies animals.
8. Taxidermy deals with the stuffing of dead animals (Taxidermy).

TWADDLE

This is a game for three or more players, though it works best with about four or five. The game really does call for a creative mind and the ability to think quickly. For each round, one player takes the chair and umpires the game. The object of the game is to talk nonsense about a topic for one minute. This is much harder than it sounds.

Start by devising a list of topics and writing these on slips of paper. The slips are folded and put in some sort of container. When each player's turn comes, a slip is chosen at random. The player then has twenty seconds to prepare a speech. There are some basic rules that must be followed:

⊙ No hesitation. If a player hesitates, any other player may call out 'Hesitation' and, if the umpire agrees, the player loses her turn.

⊙ No digression. Although the object is to talk nonsense, it must be relevant to the chosen topic. A player who digresses may be challenged and, if the umpire judges the challenge to be fair, the player loses her turn.

⊙ No repetition. You can't get away with saying the same thing in different ways. If players feel that a fellow player is doing this and the umpire agrees, she loses her turn.

DONKEY

- No frivolous challenges. If a player makes a challenge that the umpire considers unfounded, that player loses five points.

- A player who completes the whole minute gets ten points.

Here are some suggested topics to get you started:

- Irrigation projects on the Moon.

- Some uses for old yoghurt pots.

- Does toast always land butter-side down?

- Why is a tiger like a humming bird?

- The reason that a fish really does need a bicycle.

This is a game for two or more players (it works best with half a dozen or so). The game is simple to learn, but requires a good vocabulary and as much ingenuity as you can muster. A dictionary is useful for settling disputes.

This is how you play:

- The players sit in a circle. Each player starts the game with three lives.

- The first player thinks of a word of six or more letters.

- He calls out the first letter of the word.

- The next player clockwise now has to think of a word beginning with that letter and calls out the second letter of the word he has thought of.

- The third player has to think of a word beginning with the first two letters that have been called out, and he calls out the third letter of the word.

- The game continues in this way with each player adding a new letter when his turn comes.

- The trick is that you must not be the person to finish a word. If you do finish a word, you lose one of your lives. The player to keep going the longest wins.

ADVERTISING

This game can be played by two to eight people. It is based on the sort of advertisement that is rather coy about what the product advertised is actually used for.

You know how adverts for loo paper, condoms, feminine hygiene products and cream to put on embarrassing itches always have to avoid any direct mention of the purpose of the product? Well, the object of this game is to write an ad for some strange product that avoids any direct mention of what the product is or what it does.

Start by compiling a list of products. These can be quite ordinary things, such as rubber gloves or pot scourers; or, if you want to give your players a real challenge, make up fantasy products such as moonbeams or horse feathers. The products are written on slips of paper and placed in a container. Each player takes a slip at random, and then everyone has five minutes (or whatever time you consider reasonable) to come up with some advertising copy, a slogan or even a picture. Once the time is up, the players take turns to show their adverts. The other players must try to guess the name of the product being advertised. Marks out of 100 are awarded for wit and creativity. The more oblique the adverts are, the better. Any direct mention of the product and its use results in disqualification.

Here is an example of how the game might work:

Player 1 thinks of DECENT and calls out 'D'.
Player 2 thinks of DAINTY and calls out 'A'.
Player 3 thinks of DAMAGE and calls out 'M'.
Player 1 thinks of DAMPEN and calls out 'P'.
Player 2 thinks of DAMPER and calls out 'E'.
Player 3 has no alternative but to call out 'D', 'N' or 'R' and complete the word.

A player must have a valid word in mind when adding a letter. He can be challenged by another player who suspects that he is bluffing. If challenged, a player must declare the word he had in mind. If he can't do so, or if the word is not valid, he loses a life. A player can also lose a life if he waits too long before calling out a letter.

CONSEQUENCES

You probably played this game at parties as a child. For adults, however, it can be a great spur to creative thought. But be careful not to lose the spirit of fun that pervades the children's version – fun and creativity go hand in hand.

Each player needs a pen and a sheet of paper. The purpose of the game is to compose little stories to which each player contributes without knowing what the other players have written. The random nature of the contributions produces interesting results. For each part of the story, the player is told what sort of information to include – for example a male character, a female

character, where they met, what they did etc. After each player has completed a section of the story, the paper is folded over so that the next player has no idea what has been written. The sheets are passed from one player to another in a circle so that everyone gets a chance to contribute to each story. When every player has contributed to each piece of paper, the papers are gathered together and the stories read out. The required pieces of information can be anything you like. However, the following are traditionally used:

⊙ A female character.

⊙ A male character.

⊙ Where they met.

⊙ What he did.

⊙ What she did.

⊙ What he said.

⊙ What she said.

⊙ What the consequence was.

PICTURE CONSEQUENCES

This is another game that you may have played when young. It is fun for kids but can also be played by adults as an aid to creative thought. It's a good way to get people loosened up before you try to get some serious creative work out of them. For example, if you are going to run a brainstorming session, it might be an idea to relax people with a silly game of this sort.

Each player has a pencil and a piece of paper folded into thirds. The first player draws a head on the top third of the paper. The neck should just go into the second section of paper so that Player 2 knows where to start. The head portion is folded over so that it is no longer visible and Player 2 then draws a body. Again, it should go just over the bottom border so that Player 3 knows where to start. The body section is folded out of sight and Player 3 is invited to contribute legs (or flippers, wheels or even a spring for that matter). Finally, the paper is opened out and everyone gets to see the complete picture. The adult version of the game can be made more fun by choosing a theme. For example, decide that the picture is to be of a dancer, a millionaire or a space alien.

TINY TALES

This is an excellent exercise and very difficult to do well. There can be any number of players. The object of the game is to compose a short story in five minutes (or whatever time you feel is reasonable). You can vary the game as much as you like by introducing rules that make it more difficult.

Sample rules

- The story must refer to three colours.

- No word in the story must have more than three letters.

- No word can contain the letter 'E'.

- Every word must start with a vowel.

- The words must begin with the letters of the alphabet in order (i.e. the first word begins with 'A', the second with 'B' etc).

- Introduce a rule that the story must be a palindrome (must read the same forwards and backwards).

Here is an example of a story that uses only words of three letters or fewer:

A boy had a bug in a box. It ate all he fed it. One day the bug bit the boy so the boy hit the bug. The bug was ill. Now it is a bed bug.

CHESS CHALLENGES

If you think of chess as a boring game for boffins, you may be pleasantly surprised by the variations described in this section. As long as you can play a basic game of chess at beginner level, here are some great opportunities for you to think creatively.

If, on the other hand, you are a serious chess player, don't be too quick to dismiss these games as not worthy of your attention. They may not be chess as you know it, but they do provide interesting challenges that will bring real rewards in terms of boosting your creative powers.

HIGH-SPEED CHESS

- This game is played exactly like the normal game with one important exception: you get only five seconds to make your move!

- This game deprives players of the opportunity to indulge in long analyses of the game and forces quick decisions based largely on intuition.

- The results are always interesting, and experienced chess players often find themselves at the mercy of less skilled but quicker-thinking adversaries.

- The winner is the player who can call 'Checkmate'.

LOSING CHESS

- The object of this game is simply to lose all your pieces.

- In this game, the king has no special status and can be taken just like any other piece.

- A player who is able to take a piece must do so. The first player to get rid of all his pieces is the winner.

REFUSAL CHESS

- This is just like normal chess except that at each move, a player has the right to refuse the move of his adversary and insist that he play some other move instead.

- The right of refusal may be exercised as many times as one likes during the game, but only one refusal is permitted per move.

KNIGHT ERRANT CHESS

- This is played just like normal chess, except that each player has an extra knight at his disposal.

- At any point during the game, the player whose turn it is may place his extra knight on any vacant square on the board. This counts as his move.

- After the knight has been placed, it simply continues to function like a normal knight.

- As you only get one chance to place your extra knight, the skill comes in deciding at which point in the game it will do you the most good.

DOUBLE JEOPARDY CHESS

- This is played like the normal game except that each player gets two moves at a time.

- A player who gives check on his first move must forfeit his second move.

- A player who is in check must use his first move to get out of check.

GENIUS CHESS

- This version really sorts out the heavyweight thinkers from the rest. You will need to cultivate an almost superhuman ability to think ahead.

- White starts with the usual one move.

- Black then gets two moves.

- White has three moves.

- Black has four moves, etc.

- When a player gives check this ends his turn and he forfeits the rest of his moves.

- A player who is in check must get out of check on his first move.

RANDOM CHESS

Random chess is just like normal chess except that at the beginning of the game, the pieces on the first rank are arranged in a random manner (which must be the same for both players). So, for example, you could have king, rook, bishop, queen, bishop, rook, knight, knight. This does strange and terrible things, especially to the opening of the game.

AND FINALLY

Why not try inventing a completely new game using a standard chess set? The object of the game and the moves of the pieces can all be altered to suit you. Who knows, you might end up producing the next craze to sweep the games market.

MATCH POINTS

There are numerous games with matches that call for a creative approach. Here are a few especially interesting ones.

MATCHING BRIDGES

- This is a game for two players that requires pencil, paper and ten matches.
- First, draw six parallel lines on the paper. These lines should be about the same length as a match and slightly less than match-length apart.
- Each player starts with five matches and, at each turn, one match is played. A player may place a match on top of one of the parallel lines or, if two adjacent lines are occupied by matches, she can bridge the gap by laying a match across the two of them.
- A pair of matches may only be bridged once.
- A player scores one point each time she plays a match on to a line next to a line that is already occupied by a match, and two points each time she forms a bridge between two matches.
- The player with the most points when all the matches have been played is the winner.

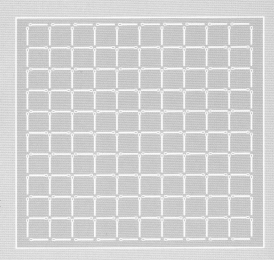

LITTLE BOXES

The matches are laid out in a 10 x 10 grid as shown above. Each player takes turns to remove either a single match, or she may remove any two matches that are touching (either in a straight line or at right angles). The player who takes the final match is the winner.

MATCH TOWER

- For this game you need an empty wine bottle and a large supply of matches.
- You must use only ONE hand when you play.
- Players take turns to place matches across the mouth of the bottle.
- Of course, once you have laid about seven matches in this way, there will be no more room, so you will have to start to set matches on top of the ones already covering the mouth of the bottle.
- A tower will start to form as more and more matches are added.
- The player to upset the tower is the loser.

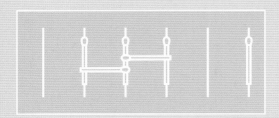

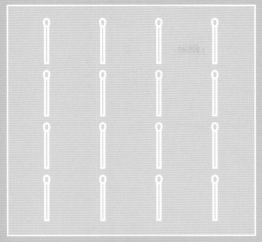

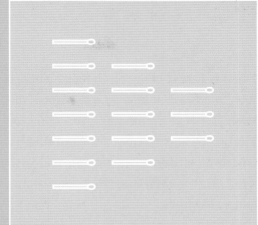

TAC TIX

This game was invented by a Danish mathematician called Piet Hein. Arrange your matches in a square like the one shown above. Each player in turn has to take one or more matches from any one row or column, but the matches taken must be adjacent, with no gaps in between. If, for example, the first player takes all four matches from the third row, the second player can take any number from adjacent rows, but he is not able to take three matches from any of the remaining columns because there is now a gap. He is only able to take matches from above or below the gap. The winner of this game is the player who forces his opponent to take the last match.

NIM

This is a game for two players. It is one of the oldest match games and may have originated in China. You start with three rows of matches – seven matches in the first row, five in the second, and three in the third. Play is by turns. Each player has to pick up any number of matches from any of the rows. She may pick up just one match, or the whole row, or any number in between. She may take from only one row at a time. The winner is the player who picks up the last match.

You can play a variant of the game by making the winner the person who forces her opponent to pick up the last match. You can also make the game more interesting by increasing the number of rows and the number of matches in each row.

HEX

For this game, you need to make a board like the one in our diagram below (the easiest way would be to scan or photocopy the diagram and blow it up to whatever size you want). You will also need 122 counters, half of them black and half white.

Hex was the invention of Piet Hein, a Danish mathematician. At first sight, it seems to be a very simple game. As you can see, the board is diamond shaped and made up of hexagons. A standard board has eleven hexagons along each side, but there is nothing to stop you from experimenting with boards of different sizes. Two sides of the board belong to Black and two to White. The four corners belong to both players.

At the start of the game, the board is empty. Black plays first and must place a counter in one of the vacant hexagons. The players place counters by turns. The objective is simply to connect the two sides of your own colour with a continuous line of counters. The winning line can twist and turn as much as necessary, as long as there are no gaps in it.

This may seem childishly simple, but the tactics needed are quite complex. Black should have the advantage in placing the first counter but, so far, no one has come up with a way for Black to use this advantage to win.

TANGRAM GAMES

Tangram is an ancient puzzle from China. To make the pieces, take a square of card, mark it as shown in the diagram, then cut along the lines so that you end up with seven pieces.

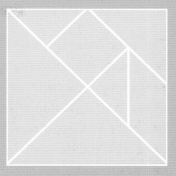

There are literally hundreds of pictures that can be made from the tangram set, and you can have hours of fun seeing how many different ones you can make. Just to get you started, try this challenge. Use the pieces to make all the digits from 1 to 8. This is not hugely difficult, but it will take a bit of thought and ingenuity to produce all of them.

⊙ Answer on page 125.

PENTOMINOES

This game was invented by the American mathematician Solomon Golomb. He thought that if dominoes could be defined as two squares joined along their edges, you could produce what he called 'polynominoes'. These would be shapes formed by connected squares. He described a single square as a monomino, two connected squares as a domino, three squares as a tromino, four squares as a teromino and five squares as a pentomino. He found that pentominoes were particularly useful because they lent themselves to games and puzzles.

There are twelve ways in which five squares can be joined to form a pentomino. These make up a set of pentominoes, as you can see from the diagram below. You can easily make yourself a set out of stiff card. Make your squares the same size as those on a standard chessboard (you'll see why later).

Once you have made the pentominoes, there are some interesting challenges you can try. For example, using all twelve pentominoes, make the following:

⊙   A 5 x 12 rectangle.

⊙   A 6 x 10 rectangle.

⊙   A 4 x 15 rectangle.

⊙   A 3 x 20 rectangle.

Another popular game is to choose just one of the pieces, and then use another nine (of the remaining eleven) to make a large-scale replica of the chosen piece. The replica will be three times the height, and three times the length, of the original. It is possible to come up with a solution for each of the twelve pentominoes.

If you have a chessboard, there is another pentomino game you can play. You need to play this with someone else. Each player in turn picks up one of the pentominoes and places it on the chessboard to cover five vacant squares. The last player to be able to place a piece on the board is the winner. It may sound simple but, trust me, it will take all your ingenuity.

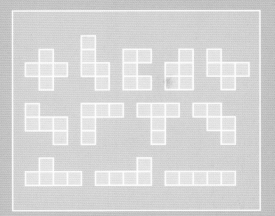

WORD LADDERS PALINDROMES

This game was invented by Lewis Carroll of _Alice in Wonderland_ fame. The idea is very simple. You take two words, one of which goes at the top of your ladder and the other at the bottom. You then have to convert the top word into the bottom one by changing one letter at each rung of the ladder. Each step must contain a proper word. Here are some examples.

You can change **HEAD** to **TAIL** like this:

HEAD   HEAL   TEAL   TELL   TALL TAIL

PIG can be converted into **STY** like this:

PIG   WIG   WAG   WAY   SAY   STY

The creative aspect of this game comes from trying to change one word into another in as few steps as possible. Once you've found a solution that works, try to find an even shorter one.

Now see what you make of the following:

WHEAT into **BREAD.**

FOUR into **FIVE.**

CAT into **DOG.**

HAND into F**OOT.**

BLACK into **WHITE.**

MORE into **LESS.**

◉ Answer on page 125.

Palindrome are phrases that read the same backwards as they do forwards. They are difficult to create and demand much ingenuity and imagination, which makes them perfect material for a creativity game. The simplest sort of palindrome simply reverses the order of whole words. Here, for example, is an epitaph from a churchyard in Cornwall.

SHALL WE ALL DIE? WE SHALL DIE ALL;

ALL DIE SHALL WE – DIE ALL WE SHALL.

Even a palindrome of this type is quite hard to produce, but the best palindromes are those where the whole thing can be reversed. There are many famous palindromes. This one is attributed to Napoleon:

'ABLE WAS I 'ERE I SAW ELBA.'

Here are some others that will help you get into the right mindset:

SAD? I'M MIDAS.

DENNIS AND EDNA SINNED.

NOW, NED, I AM A MAIDEN NUN; NED, I AM A MAIDEN WON.

SNUG & RAW WAS I 'ERE I SAW WAR & GUNS.

SUMS ARE NOT SET AS A TEST ON ERASMUS.

SEX AT NOON TAXES.

LIVE NOT ON EVIL.

CRYPTARITHMS

You will see that the meaning of palindromes is not their most important feature. They frequently sound rather odd, particularly as they get longer, for example the following:

A NEW ORDER BEGAN, A MORE ROMAN AGE BRED ROWENA.

DOC, NOTE. I DISSENT. A FAST NEVER PREVENTS A FATNESS. I DIET ON COD.

DEGAS, ARE WE NOT DRAWN ONWARD, WE FREER FEW, DRAWN ONWARD TO NEW ERAS AGED?

Palindromes are, for obvious reasons concerned with people called Bob, Anna, Pip and Ada. They also make use of the '&' symbol, which gets the composer off a rather awkward hook.

This is a game you can play on your own or with friends, and at any time you please. Usually, the winner is the person who creates the longest palindrome.

This is another type of puzzle that may inspire creativity in people with an ingenious streak. In a cryptarithm, letters are substituted for numbers in a mathematical calculation. So, for example, you might get one like this:

S	E	N	D		M	O	R	E
G	O	L	D		M	O	N	E	Y

When you manage to work out the values of the letters, you get a sum that looks like this:

5	4	7	8		1	6	2	4
9	6	3	8		1	6	7	4	0

Once you understand the principle you can start to make ever more complicated puzzles. For example: **TWO X TWO = THREE** can be calculated as: **138 X 138 = 19044**

Writers of cryptarithms enjoy making their puzzles all the wittier by using words in which the meaning is significant. Here is one composed by the famous puzzle-writer H. E. Dudeney. It illustrates how, contrary to the proverb, two wrongs can make a right:

W	R	O	N	G
W	R	O	N	G
R	I	G	H	T

2	5	9	3	8
2	5	9	3	8
5	1	8	7	6

REBUSES

A rebus uses pictures, numbers and letters to make words and sentences. Usually, the solution to the rebus will be some well-known phrase, though this does not always have to be the case.

Here is one that was once known to all schoolchildren:

Y	Y	U	R
Y	Y	U	B
I	C	U	R
Y	Y	4	ME

The translation goes like this:

Too wise you are,
Too wise you be,
I see you are,
Too wise for me.

This is another famous one:

HILL
JOHN
HANTS

What does it mean? It is actually an address:
John Underhill, Andover, Hants

Here are some modern examples:

KNEE
LIGHT

This translates as *'neon light'*.

STAND
I

This can be read as *'I understand'*.

P
O
U
R

This translates as *'downpour'*.

One of my favourites is this:

NHAPPY

It took me quite some time to tumble to the solution – *'Unhappy without you'*.

Composing rebuses is fun and gives you great scope to be creative. It teaches you to think about words and pictures in unorthodox and interesting new ways. Give it a try. Take any familiar phrase and see if you can come up with a witty and amusing rebus to illustrate it.

HIDDEN NUMBERS

LIPOGRAMS

It is quite easy to find numbers hidden in words. For example, **'WEIGHT'** contains **'EIGHT'**, and **'FIVE'** is lurking in **'VERIFY'**. The point of this game is to come up with the shortest possible word that contains each number. For example, you can get **'ONE'** from **'WONDER'**, but you get more credit for getting it from **'STONE'** and even more if you managed to come up with **'EON'**. You can't use words that are too similar to the original (for example, getting **'FIVE'** out of **'FIVER'** is cheating). Now, try to find the shortest words that contain the following numbers.

A lipogram is a piece of text that deliberately eschews the use of one or more letters. Here, for example, is what *Mary Had a Little Lamb* would look like without the use of the letter 'S'.

Mary had a little lamb,
With fleece a pale white hue,
And everywhere that Mary went
The lamb kept her in view;
To academe he went with her,
Illegal, and quite rare;
It made the children laugh and play
To view a lamb in there.

Some lipograms are easier than others. If, for example, you want to eliminate all mention of the letter 'A' in the Mary poem, you are forced to cheat a little by giving the girl a name change.

One	Two	Three
Four	Five	Six
Seven	Eight	Nine
Ten	Eleven	Twelve
Thirteen	Fourteen	Fifteen
Sixteen	Seventeen	Eighteen
Nineteen	Twenty	Thirty
Thirty-one	Thirty-six	Thirty-seven
Thirty-nine	Forty	Forty-one
Fifty	Fifty-one	Fifty-nine
Sixty	Sixty-three	Seventy
Eighty	Eighty-one	Ninety
Ninety-one	Ninety-nine	One hundred

Suzie owned one little sheep,
Its fleece shone white like snow,
Every region where Suzy went
The sheep did surely go,
He followed her to school one time,
Which broke the rigid rule;
The children frolicked in their room,
To see the sheep in school.

Now try to come up with lipograms of your own. You can use any piece of text you like but you will get the most fun (and the most creative exercise) if you try eliminating different letters by turn from the same text.

⊙ Answer on page 125.

PART FOUR:
USING CREATIVITY
TO MAKE A LIVING

A lot of the work involved in creativity is interesting and fun. This is why so many people are determined to pursue a career in some form of creative activity.

Creative work, however, does have its less glamorous side (and the pay in certain areas is poor). As long as you are producing work just for yourself, you can mess about in any way you choose, but as soon as you want to launch your ideas commercially, the rules change. Now you have to impress people enough to get them to part with hard cash in return for your creative skills. Before approaching anyone for financial backing, there are a number of issues that you need to consider.

'I have traveled the length and breadth of this country and talked with the best people, and I can assure you that data processing is a fad that won't last out the year.'

THE EDITOR IN CHARGE OF BUSINESS BOOKS FOR PRENTICE HALL, 1957

THE UNGLAMOROUS BITS

There is a popular image of the creative person as a wild, freedom-loving, spontaneous individual who annoys all the stuffy suit-wearers by coming up with brilliant ideas in an unconventional way.

This has given a lot of people the excuse to behave in a free and easy way in the name of creativity. The truth is not so simple. There are people who manage to combine an unfettered lifestyle with creativity, but they are nowhere near as numerous in real life as they are in popular myth. There are plenty of people who lead what they fondly imagine to be a creative life, but most of them are creating nothing of any monetary value. The ones who do manage to combine a productive career with a carefree artistic lifestyle usually have a team of managers who do all the nitty-gritty for them.

TIME

Would-be creatives have to learn the importance of time management. When you are involved in any creative project, one of the worst things is to be oblivious to time. If you wait for inspiration to strike, or if you don't happen to feel in the right creative mood on a particular day, you'll end up achieving nothing. It is far, far better to work at a project doggedly and then at a later date decide which bits to keep and which to throw out. At least if you have come up with something, however bad it may be, you have material to work with and improve. If you've produced nothing, you're no further forward.

When starting a creative project, it is vital to work out if you can complete it in a reasonable amount of time (or if you are fulfilling a commission, whether you can meet the deadline). It is mystifying how so many people do not perform the simple mathematical operation of dividing the amount of work to be done by their rate of work, and then see whether it fits into the time available for the project. This is absolutely fundamental and if you don't do it, and don't make a serious attempt to stick to the work rate you've decided upon, your project stands every chance of being a failure.

If you are working in a team, one member of that team needs to be the project manager, responsible for nagging and chivvying the others to keep to schedule. This is often an unpopular job, but it has to be done. The best type of project manager gets results by inspiring enthusiasm in the rest of the team. More usually, project managers merely nag everyone to death until they get the required results. This may not be very pleasant, but it is necessary.

If you work alone, you need to be your own project manager, and this calls for huge amounts of self-discipline. Construct a timetable for your project and set realistic targets. Always build in a bit of contingency time for things to go wrong (which they always do). Learn to be brutally honest with yourself: it's no good thinking that if you get a bit behind you'll be able to make up the time later, because you probably won't.

If you are hoping to sell your creative skills, you will quickly discover that buyers want reliability above all else. You may produce stunningly creative output, but if you are unreliable, you'll soon find that clients stop using you. In business parlance, they want 'deliverables', which simply means that you produce what you promised, when you promised it and at the price you agreed. If you can't or won't do any of these things, then unless you are one of a tiny band of genuine creative geniuses whose work is unique, you will soon be unemployed.

MONEY

If you are planning a project you need to know the answers to two things with great clarity: a) How much money will you need? b) Where is the money coming from? The first question is answered by producing a budget. This can consist of no more than a single sheet of paper or it can be a long, complex document. In either case what matters is that when you have finished your budget it should be as accurate as you can make it and should take account of all possible eventualities. If you are wise you will also include a contingency fund to deal with unforeseen problems that will almost certainly arise. With a complicated budget it is tempting to let a professional take over and run it for you. But remember – finance is the real guts of any project. If you don't understand the exact financial position then you are no longer in control of the project.

Who provides the money? Ideally you would finance your project yourself but this is seldom possible. You will need investors, but the trouble with that is that anyone who invests money in your project is entitled to some control over the way things are run. The more money they invest, the bigger say they will demand. The danger is that you will end up as little better than hired help on your own project. Some people get around the problem by getting family and friends to loan them money. This can work very well but supposing your project fails? How do you tell your Mum, Dad and Great Aunt Hattie that you just lost their money? So before you start work you must reach a detailed written agreement with your investors about how much they are investing.

STRUCTURE

You will have to communicate your idea to others, and therefore it needs to be clearly comprehensible. Just as there are people who feel that a disregard for time makes them look like creative geniuses, there are also people (often the same ones) who feel that they should be able to present their work to people in a raw state, and let them pick the bones out of it. Nothing could be further from the truth. The sort of people who buy creative work (publishers, TV producers, advertising executives, newspaper editors, etc.) do not expect to have to struggle to understand it. Nor do they expect to read through long, tedious explanations in order to take in what they are being shown. These are very busy people who are constantly being bombarded with projects from eager creatives. They like short, sharp, clear explanations, preferably in brief bullet points. If they like your idea, they will ask to see it in more detail, but in the first instance it has to be boiled down to its essence. This is, in any case, a good exercise, because unless you can grasp the core of your idea and understand why other people should be interested in it, you don't stand much chance of explaining it to anyone else.

The structure of your proposal must follow a clear and logical order. It is essential that all parts of the presentation hang together properly and can be easily followed by anyone of average intelligence. (This bit is important – never overestimate the intelligence of the people who will be evaluating your idea. You would not believe just how many truly stupid people get into positions for which they are utterly unqualified.) Unless you make your work idiot-proof, you run the risk of being misunderstood. As the author Douglas Adams put it, 'A common mistake that people make when trying to design something completely foolproof is to underestimate the ingenuity of complete fools.'

In some industries (cinema and advertising, for example) it is normal to present an idea as a storyboard with a series of pictures illustrating the various parts of the idea. This is an excellent technique and can be applied to all sorts of projects. It has the merit that you can use pictures to convey a lot of information in very little space.

Before you try selling your idea to someone else, try it out on someone you know whose opinion you trust. I've worked with TV people who would never go into a presentation with real TV channel executives without first having set up a dummy presentation in which they get someone from outside the project to offer criticism and point out areas that are too vague or weak. It is a very rare idea that cannot be improved by a bit of constructive criticism from friends.

PRESENTATION

It is vital that any idea being presented to potential buyers or backers should look good. Dog-eared pages bearing coffee stains and corrections in ballpoint pen will not impress. Your work can be wonderful, but if it looks awful, people will usually not give it the attention it deserves. Also, remember that creative work rarely finds financial support at the first attempt. You may have to approach many potential backers before you find the one who is prepared to offer you a deal. Although it costs more money to present fresh copies of your work at each presentation, it is a false economy not to make the effort.

Picture yourself as someone who buys creative work. Your desk will always be covered with more submissions than you can ever possibly use. However, most of them are junk and can be thrown out after only a few seconds' of consideration. Of the remainder, there will be a tiny number that you can use. As you are only human and your time is limited, you will be attracted to those submissions that are clear, well presented and appealing to look at. Anything that looks tatty, or seems to have been rejected by numerous previous buyers, is likely to go straight into your reject pile.

It is not unusual for well-presented work to get more attention than it really deserves. I remember a book that circulated in a publishing company I once worked for. It claimed to find hidden meanings in the dimensions of the Great Pyramid (and that in itself should have rung some warning bells). However, the work was immaculately presented, the pages were snowy white without a single bent corner, and the illustrations had been done with enormous care and considerable artistic flair. Because of this, the book did the rounds for some weeks and came up for consideration at several meetings. It was only after some time that it started to dawn on people that this beautifully presented manuscript was in fact full of the most outrageous twaddle.

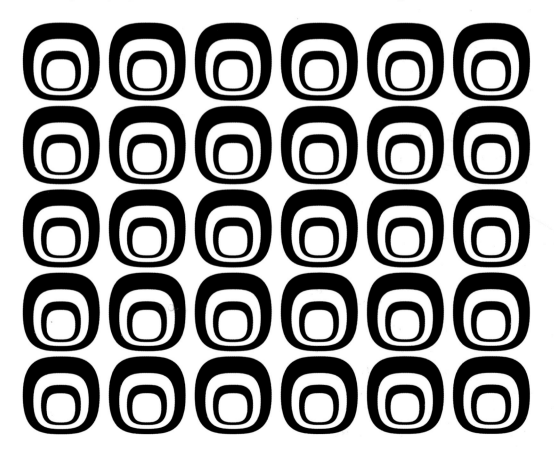

LEARNING FROM EXPERIENCE

In any form of creative work, you have to handle criticism, rejection and failure. As we have seen earlier, even some of the brightest ideas were often ridiculed and misunderstood at first. Such experiences should be regarded as a test of your self-belief.

If you can continue to pursue your aims in spite of criticism that is frequently ill-informed and unfair, you are likely to succeed in the long-term.

Not all criticism is bad, and it is very important to learn how to get the most benefit out of constructive criticism. An honest and well-meaning critic can be far more valuable to you than a friend who offers undiluted praise just because he doesn't want to hurt your feelings. Have you noticed how many authors include an acknowledgement to the skill of their editor in the finished book? The reason is that a good editor can be hugely influential in getting authors to produce their best work. The editor acts as a candid friend who enjoys the author's trust to such an extent that he can say, 'I don't think that passage works. You need to rethink it.' Creative people are deeply involved in their own projects, but are often insecure because being creative can be quite lonely. They can be fiercely protective of their work and, at the same time, very stubborn about accepting necessary changes to it. This is where the opinion of a trusted critic can be vital. Because you are so close to your own work, you simply cannot see it dispassionately enough. You need to see it through the eyes of another in order to find its flaws.

All creative work is a constant process of learning. No truly creative person ever produces a piece of work that cannot be bettered. Of course, there comes a point when the picture is painted, the novel written or the invention patented – and these points are endings of a sort. But they do not represent an end to the learning process, because that goes on as long as the originator lives.

Failure plays a large part in the learning process. As we have seen, most creative ideas end in failure. There is no shame in this; it is simply the way the world works. To get a few good ideas, you need to produce a lot of duff ones. It is, however, important not to brush away the failed ideas as quickly as possible. It may be painful to look at our failures and consider what went wrong, but it is vitally important that we do so. Every failure is a lesson in what we should or should not do next time. If you refuse to learn the lesson, you stand a good chance of repeating the mistake.

THE WELL RUNS DRY

The fund of creative ideas available to us is sometimes likened to a well. We dip into it again and again trying to draw inspiration and, although sometimes all we come up with is a piece of rubbish, if we keep trying we usually find what we are seeking. But does the well ever run dry? Certainly, many creative people do experience periods when ideas do not flow easily – the well-known phenomenon of 'writer's block' is an example. When this happens, it can be very hard to get the flow started again. This is why so many creative people resort to extreme methods to try to revive their flagging powers.

If you find that the ideas just won't come the first rule is 'Don't panic'. Everyone has times when they feel uninspired. First you must ask yourself why you feel as you do. It may be that you have worked on a project for so long that you have become stale and need to take time off. At this point you can either take a holiday in the hope that the rest will give your mind the time it needs to revitalize itself. Alternatively you can try to switch to another project that calls for you to be creative in a different way. You will find that this will often not only restore your confidence in your ability but will also allow

you eventually to return to the original project with renewed enthusiasm.

If no matter what you do the ideas just refuse to flow you need to consider whether there is some other cause. Maybe you have other worries that are sapping your strength or perhaps you have some problem with your health that you have been too busy to deal with. It helps to talk the problem over with someone who is close to you. They may have noticed a change in your behaviour and have some idea of what is causing it. You should also ask yourself whether there is some aspect of the project that is bothering you and causing your creativity to dry up.

Drying up of creative powers is almost always a temporary condition so it is important not to worry about it too much. Getting stressed about it will only make matters worse. Try to stay calm and you will find that in due course your inspiration will come back.

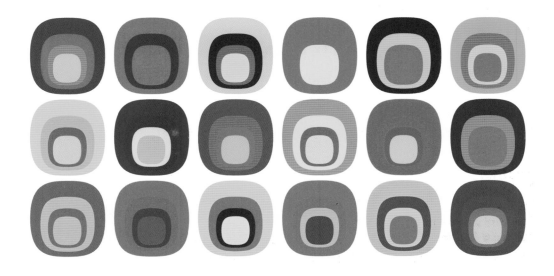

ANSWERS

CREATIVE, OR JUST PLAIN NUTS?

See page 9.

He took one nut off each of the other wheels and added them to the defective wheel. Each wheel then had four nuts, and that way it was sufficiently safe to drive to a garage and get some more nuts.

THE ABSENT AUNT

See page 32.

The sisters were identical twins.

DEATH OF THE DEALER

See page 32.

He couldn't arrest any of the men – but the dealer was a woman. He arrested her.

LAST SUPPER

See page 32.

Mickey was a pet mouse who had escaped and been caught in a mousetrap.

ODD ANIMALS

See page 33.

None of them is actually what it says it is. The koala is not a bear, the Bombay duck is not a duck and so on.

SEA STORY

See page 33.

The vessel was Apollo 11, which landed in the Sea of Tranquillity on the Moon.

SUCCESSFUL PLAYERS

See page 33.

They were a band employed to play background music.

POLITICAL PROBLEMS

See page 33.

They were still in the tin.

THREE SHORT PLANKS

See page 34.

Task 1

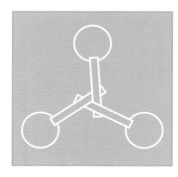

Task 2

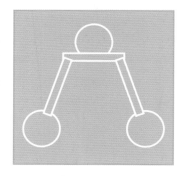

DOTTY DILEMMA

See page 35.

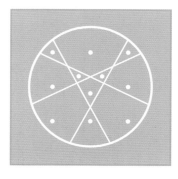

THE VANISHING SQUARE

See page 36.

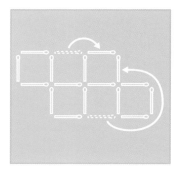

WINE WOBBLE

See page 36.

Fill the glass to the very brim. Now take a piece of card and lay it on the glass. Pressing the glass against the card with your fingers, turn the whole thing upside down. Now take your hand away from the card. Atmospheric pressure will ensure that the water stays where it is. Put the inverted glass on a table and very carefully pull out the card. If anyone now tries to pick up the glass, the water will immediately be released.

MATCH PLAY

See page 37.

THE HOLE STORY

See page 38.

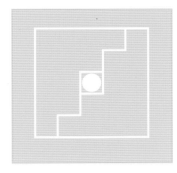

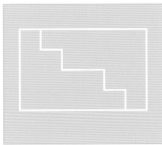

THE PUZZLING PRINCESS

See page 38.

Yasmin said, 'You will feed me to the vultures.' If that is true she should be eaten by the genie, but if it's false she should be fed to the vultures. The genie was stuck in a paradox where it was impossible to work out the correct punishment.

MAZE MYSTERY

See page 39.

Keep your right hand touching the bushes on the right-hand side of the path.

WHICH LIST?

See page 39.

The words in list A are all anagrams of girls' names (Mary, May, Delia, Ruth, Lisa). The words in list B are boys' names (Eric, Andrew, Steven, Lee, Cyril). YACHT is an anagram of Cathy, so it goes with list A.

NO WAY BACK

See page 40.

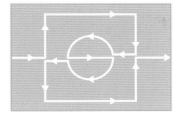

ORIGINAL ORIGAMI

See page 40.

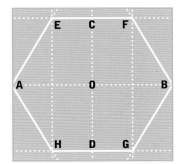

First, fold the paper in half horizontally and vertically, making the lines AOB and COD. You can then get EH and FG by folding the edges to the centre-line COD. In the process, you bisect AO and OB. Fold AJ so that J lies on the line EH at point E. Do the same with the other corners and you will get the points F, G and H. All you have to do after that is to fold AE, EF, FB, BG, GH and HA. Now you have a hexagon: AEFBGH.

DIVIDING THE DISC

See page 41.

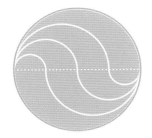

SHELL SHOCK

See page 41.

If you rap the knife sharply on the table, the eggshell will simply bounce off the blade and will not be pierced. The trick is to loosen your grip on the knife a split second before it hits the table. It will then bounce in your hand and penetrate the shell.

COIN CONUNDRUM

See page 42.

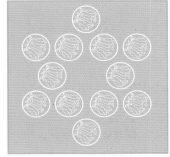

TOO MANY SQUARES

See page 42.

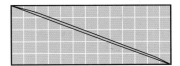

If you try to work this out just by looking at diagrams A and B, you'll never solve this puzzle. If, however, you make the thing for yourself out of paper, you'll see that when you assemble the rectangle there is a small gap along the long diagonal line. The gap has the same area as one square. This diagram exaggerates the gap so that you can see it. Actually it is tiny and, unless you are wide awake, you might easily miss it.

HUMILIATION!

See page 43.

Each line describes the one

above it. So, it's: 1, then one 1, then two 1s, then one 2 and one 1, and so on. The final row is 31131211131221.

CENTURY CONUNDRUM

See page 43.

BERMUDA TRIANGLES
PUZZLE 1

See page 44.
Thirteen. Add all the numbers and put the sum in the centre of the triangle.

PUZZLE 2

See page 45.
Twelve. Multiply the top number by the one on the bottom left, then add the one at bottom right. Place the result in the centre.

PUZZLE 3

See page 45.
Fourteen. Multiply the bottom numbers and subtract the top one. The result is, as before, placed in the centre.

PUZZLE 4

See page 45.
Seventeen. Multiply the top number by the one on the bottom right, then add the one on the bottom left. The results, however, have been put not in their own triangle but in a neighbouring one.

PUZZLE 5

See page 46.
Nine. Add all the numbers. Swap the results between the first and fourth triangles, and the second and third.

PUZZLE 6

See page 46.
The answer is 0. You probably didn't take long to work out that the letters can be converted into numbers according to their position in the alphabet (i.e. A = 1, B = 2, C = 3 and so on, to Z = 26). Once you know that, it is fairly easy to work out that all the numbers for each triangle have been added, converted back into letters, and then placed in neighbouring triangles.

PUZZLE 7

See page 46.
Twelve. Using alphanumeric values, add the bottom numbers and subtract the top one. When placing the results, swap the first and third triangles, and the second and fourth.

PUZZLE 8

See page 47.
Were you sufficiently on the ball to see that this puzzle was entirely different? If not, you will be irked to know that the letters have no numerical significance. They spell 'CAUGHT YOU OUT'. Did I?

TRANSPLANTATION

See page 48.

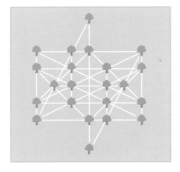

PAPER PUZZLE

See page 48.
Make a loop out of the paper. Before you join the ends, give one of them a half-turn twist. This will then create one of those strange geometrical oddities that has only one side.

CASH PROBLEM

See page 48.

DEAD END

See page 49.
There are 91,520 possible readings!

MATCH MYSTERY

See page 49.

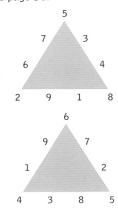

TRIANGLE TOTALS

See page 50.

CUP CONUNDRUM

See page 50.

Tie the cup using a bow, then cut through both loops of the bow and, of course, the cup will stay put.

CHAIR CHALLENGE

See page 50.

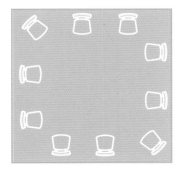

HANKY PANKY

See page 50.

First, ram the handkerchief into the tumbler as hard as you can. Then invert the tumbler and push it quickly into the water, keeping it completely upright as you do so. The air in the tumbler will be trapped and will prevent any water from reaching the handkerchief.

QUILT QUESTION

See page 51.

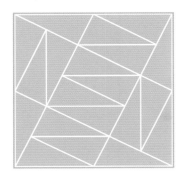

JUMBLED LETTERS

See page 51.

The letters will make the phrase 'JUST ONE WORD'!

BEHEADINGS

See page 68.

1 Table / able. 2 Wall / all.
3 Mutter / utter. 4 Flung / lung.
5 Lamp / amp. 6 Clover / lover.
7 Orange / range. 8 Frank / rank.
9 Bark / ark. 10 Taunt / aunt.
11 Pink / ink. 12 Silk / ilk.

NOW TRY THIS

See page 69.

The question refers to someone taking off a pair of gloves. Ten fingers are taken away, but of course ten remain.

CONCENTRATION

See page 83.

ROUND 1

Eleven pairs.
E G; G I; N P; T V; V X; K M;
M O; O Q; F H; H J; J L

ROUND 2

Thirteen pairs.
6 4; 8 2; 5 5; 4 6; 6 4; 9 1;
2 8; 6 4; 9 1; 2 8; 4 6; 6 4

ROUND 3

Twelve pairs.
D G; L O; O R; R U; J M;
M P; T W; F I; I L; L O; W Z

ROUND 4

Nine sets of three.
5 2 5; 4 6 2; 2 9 0; 3 7 2;
2 4 6; 4 6 2; 4 5 3; 2 8 2;
2 4 6; 4 6 2

ROUND 5

There are over 640 correct routes.

TANGRAM GAMES

See page 109.

WORD LADDERS

See page 110.

WHEAT CHEAT CHEAM
CREAM BREAM BREAD
FOUR FOUL FOOL FOOT
FORT FORE FIRE FIVE
CAT COT DOT DOG
HAND HARD LARD LORD
FORD FORT FOOT
BLACK SLACK STACK
STALK STALE SHALE
WHALE WHILE WHITE
MORE LORE LOSE LOSS
LESS

HIDDEN NUMBERS

See page 113.

Eon, Tow, Ether, Flour, Verify, Xis (Xi is the fourteenth letter of the Greek alphabet), Evens, Weight, Inner, Net, Leavened, Wavelet, Tethering, Counterfeit, Stiffener, Existent, Retentiveness, Heightened, Internecine, Noteworthy, Thirsty, Retinopathy, Thyrotoxicosis, Hypersensitivity, Interchangeability, Frosty, Confectionery, Stiffly, Affectionately, Inefficiently, Sexuality, Heterosexuality, Sensitively, Weighty, Homogeneity, Intently, Conveniently, Inconveniently, Uncomprehended.

INDEX

PICTURE ACKNOWLEDGEMENTS

Chrysalis Books Group Plc is committed to respecting the intellectual property rights of others. We have therefore taken all reasonable efforts to ensure that the reproduction of all content on these pages is done with the full consent of copyright owners. If you are aware of any unintentional omissions please contact the company directly so that any necessary corrections may be made for future editions.

10	© Underwood & Underwood / CORBIS
22	© Gianni Dagli Orti / CORBIS
53	© Leonard de Selva / CORBIS
55	© Bettmann / CORBIS
57	© Bettmann / CORBIS
62	© Bettmann / CORBIS
66	© Bettmann / CORBIS
70	© ML Sinibaldi / CORBIS
94	© The Illustrated London News
104	Royalty Free
119	© Digital Vision
121	© Digital Vision